GOT PURPOSE?

HEBREW GEMATRIA REVEALS ESOTERIC TRUTHS

(Answering the question, "What is life all about?")

S.E.E.

DEDICATION

With grateful appreciation, I thank **Father God** for **His** *'still small voice'* and **Holy Spirit's** leading and guidance in understanding eternal truths.

I also want to express my gratitude to my husband, John. Through our many years together, he has continued to show the courage to boldly address certain hidden truths and revelations. He has also been my most significant supporter and financier concerning all of my published books.

Finally, I wish to thank my daughter, Katrina, for her labor-intensive diligence and quality efforts in editing and publishing this work. Only by her keen, spiritually opened eyes and immeasurable faithfulness has this book become a reality.

CONTENTS

AUTHOR'S NOTE

Allow me to be honest here. At one point in my life, I felt anxious and somewhat baffled at the reality of life on this earth. Inside my head was a jumbled mess of questions without discovering any answers. "What is life all about?" This question tugged at my heartstrings.

Do you also wonder why you're alive? Do you feel that, though you try to keep focused and goal-oriented in your little corner of the world, many external occurrences beyond your control chip away at the plans for your future? Also, are those external happenings significantly disrupting the peace and calm you're trying to achieve?

Have you ever wondered about your purpose? Is something missing from your life, but you just don't know what it is? You can't put a name to it, but somewhere inside, you realize that complete happiness and settled contentment seem to elude you. It is just out of reach at every turn, though you desperately long to have it. You can only hope for a new season to come along that will finally cause you to feel established.

You sense, too, that there are some connecting pieces to this exhaustive puzzle called life that you cannot put in place. And you are troubled by the possibility that maybe, those will never be found. You've tried to figure life out, but you simply can't see the bigger picture; it is only a vague concept, a foggy haze surrounds you, and the path is not well marked.

Do you also feel you are merely bobbing around on the surface of life, not fully immersed in a refreshing stream flowing to somewhere extraordinary? Shouldn't life offer a continual refreshing and a move toward improving everything? And you seriously want to be connected to something greater than yourself. Because, otherwise, who wants to keep struggling along like this, right?

Even your very existence seems surreal at times. Like me, you probably want to believe in the supernatural; you've heard things and have been involved in a few unexplainable happenings. With my experience, I had heard about the supernatural but knew too that the depths of the supernatural are beyond one's comprehension. And, you understand that, in some small way, you surely must be part of the whole, whatever the whole happens to be. If only you could discover the perfect place where you fit?

You know that you are alive because you breathe and can feel pain. Unseen emotional distress erupts deep inside your mind, heart, and soul, and sometimes it all but overwhelms you. The stress of living is a definite fact. You cannot see it, yet you feel it. And you hope to avoid it, if at all possible. The supernatural might hold the answer to your daily misery. Still, you have so many unanswered questions before you could even get to a place to understand it, let alone live in it.

You feel love, too. But you can't see or touch it. Your physical body is a reality, possibly a result of others' love, a fact you've had no control over. Though, the truth is, here you are! Now, what do you do with yourself?

Aren't we forced to admit that we mortals are not capable of fully appreciating the magnitude of a supernatural relationship with an invisible *Being*? Although we do have the distressing thought that our spot in eternity is not secure, we almost want to run the other way, far away from the supernatural. And what a paradox that is, right? But we just don't seem wired for that!

I had been a Christian, a believer, and a reunited child of *God* for a long while; still, some things simply did not add up. From my reality to the spiritual realm, that nagging gap was like a ravine only seen through a dense fog. I was kept far apart from it; a vast distance loomed between my current reality to where I'd been taught the supernatural realm resides.

This gap is primarily because one genuinely cannot understand how a relationship with the *Highest Deity* in the heavens should unfold throughout one's daily life. Many have wrestled with these questions of otherworldly realms since the beginning of time, myself included. But are we responsible for what we do not know, have not been taught, or have never even heard mentioned? You and I are not alone in this dilemma.

Do not despair! Indeed, the whole truth has not been taught in pulpits in western culture. The fact is reality is certainly stranger than fiction. Most ministers seem comfortable dealing with natural reality, never delving too deeply into the sea of the supernatural. Sadly, some scholars cannot fathom considering the truth.

Are you ready to consider some things you have never heard of before? I am only asking you to be willing to listen to what is presented as you read, then do your own calculations and decide for yourself. Yes, actual calculations. A Mathematics Glossary is provided at the back of this book.

God Almighty's true-life story is the most remarkable love story ever told. Yet, to date, the whole has not been fully understood. In this book, you will read the rest of the story. And! You are included in ***God's*** love story to end all love stories! You will not only read about this love story but also see it written down in calculated form, with undeniable mathematical proofs, using ***God's*** perfect love language, Hebrew/Ibree.

Note: Bible references were taken from KJV Bible. Definitions/meanings were taken from Strong's Concordance, 1890's Edition, using Hebrew root words. A few references were used from the Greek section of the Strong's Concordance.

CHAPTER ONE
CONSIDERING THE UNHEARD OF

A great deal of esoteric, spiritual truths openly revealed and clarified in this book might seem strange upon your initial reading. These cryptic **Biblical** truths are not readily visible within the writings of the Old or New Testaments. Yet, these realities are there. One merely needs to be bold enough to ask the tough questions that do not make sense on the surface and then dig deeper in search of hidden truths like buried treasure. *(Isaiah 45:3 / Matthew 13:44 / 1 Corinthians 2:10)*

A few religious sects and cults have touched on some of these realities. But they eventually go on tangents, teaching twisted versions of these supernatural accuracies. There is a reason for twisted versions occurring within religious denominations. Those reasons will be addressed.

Although what you will be reading has been relatively unheard of, all will be examined and demonstrated in three different ways: words, numbers, and with **Scripture** verses. At this juncture, take a moment to consider previously unimagined events in the **Bible,** which had never happened before in the history of mankind. And yet, those indeed occurred at least once; events which most believers now readily accept as facts. **God Almighty** has an ordered plan for all of **His** creation. Still, **He** continues to perform innumerable creative deeds in the most phenomenal ways.

In ancient times, scribes penned accounts of these spectacular events after men and women received instruction from **God Almighty** on details concerning those extraordinary occurrences. Though our minds might not be able to visualize these events, being so far out and otherworldly, we should have no conflict in believing facts presented in **Scripture.** Why? Because documentation by many sources points to the **Bible** as a book that has stood the test of time and has proven its accuracy repeatedly, especially where the prophetic had been foretold: historical locations unearthed, centuries-old records of generations of reigning kings and their accomplishments, time-tested predictions that have since come to pass, and excavated artifacts that have been discovered, as well as those unusual occurrences shared by word of mouth. Case in point, accounts of Egyptian Pharaohs through the ages have produced far less documentation to certify their lives and significant feats during their reigns, yet all are widely accepted as historically accurate.

So, what about the unthinkable and the unheard of…until it happened? It's good to be reminded of miraculous events in which mankind has had the privilege of participating after receiving powerfully authoritative commissions granted by an *Almighty God,* according to *His* good pleasure and for increasing *His* kingdom on earth.

Other men, women and events could be mentioned; the following is a short list:

- א *God* creates all there ever was, is, or ever will be by speaking *His* Hebrew/Ibree language

- א The Garden of Eden is a paradise tucked away here on earth

- א Adam and Eve were forced out of the Garden of Eden by cherubim

- א And cherubim now guard the Garden of Eden so mankind cannot enter

- א Enoch was so obedient and faithful that *God* took him

- א Noah built an ark for his family when it had never rained on earth before

- א Only one family clan, Noah's, remained alive while the world flooded over

- א Noah's small family began the restoration of all mankind on this earth

- א *God* destroyed the tower of Babel

- א Many languages were simultaneously developed within each family's tribe

- א Abraham and Sarah had a child when they were 100 years old

- א Jacob, his two wives and their maidservants birthed the twelve tribes of Israel

- א Joseph went from the prison to the palace within two years

- א ***God*** told a murderer, Moses, to pronounce ten plagues on the land of Egypt

- א Pharaoh relented and allowed all two million slaves to go free at the same time

- א The Red Sea parted, and two million people walked across on dry land

- א Manna and water were provided for two million people in a desert for forty years

- א Their shoes and clothing never waxed old for forty-plus years

- א Joshua marched, sang, blew trumpets, and the city wall of Jericho fell down

- א Rahab, a harlot, trusted ***God***; the house/wall where she lived was not destroyed

- א Jonah was swallowed up by a whale and then regurgitated on dry land

- א Gideon, with an army of 300 men but no weapons, destroyed an enemy army

- א Samson killed the entire elite government of a pagan nation by pulling down a temple

- א Elijah was taken in a chariot of fire

- א Elisha's bones in a grave brought a dead man back to life

- א Shadrach, Meshach, and Abednego, inside a fiery furnace, held a meeting with ***Jesus***

- א Daniel slept with the lions

- א Deborah, judge over Israel, killed an enemy leader with her bare hands and a spike

- א Esther saved her entire nation by fasting for three days and risking her own life

- א Ruth, a widow and Gentile, became the grandmother of King David

- א David killed a lion with his bare hands

א David killed the giant, Goliath, with one smooth stone in a sling

א Mary risked her life and had a child when she had never known a man

א **Christ Jesus** performed miracles, granting authority to **His** disciples to do the same

א **Christ Jesus** ascended in the clouds after securing **Salvation** for mankind

א A murderer, Saul/Paul, received **Salvation** after meeting **Christ Jesus**.

Amazing to realize that mere mortals were commissioned to accomplish these supernatural events on this terra-firma. Supernatural occurrences did transpire on this earth, with humans being extensively involved. Reading further, you will view mathematical calculations that substantiate the supernatural adds up and makes perfect sense when dealing with the eternal spiritual realm.

Spiritual life, the real purpose for all that was created, and the reason you live on this earth are explained and substantiated without a doubt. **Scripture** verses that address various truths will astound you, and you will see with new eyes as you've never understood those verses before. Mathematical equations have been worked up from words, letters and numbers intertwined within **God Almighty's** perfect language, Hebrew/Ibree. Along with the results of these equations pointing you to the truth in the **Bible,** your purpose, your ability to live within the eternal realm here and now, and your future in the eternal kingdom will be made perfectly clear.

How closely are you tied to this world? It would be best for you to be tied to the eternal realm. Keep this in mind: *"A threefold cord is not easily broken." (Ecclesiastes 4:12)*

CHAPTER TWO
HEARING GOD'S VOICE

Let's begin at the beginning. To do this, we must first zero in on the reasons for creation and why **God Almighty** has done all that **He** has done to form this beautiful earth all around us, which we can see and touch. Fundamentally, **God Almighty** created mankind for **His** good pleasure, and this is multi-dimensional. Just like someone who took the game of chess and developed extreme chess, **God** has greater challenges for his spiritual children.

Here's an analogy of the phrase, **'God's** good pleasure.' You are a creative being, and so, you must create. It's just in your nature to do so. You decide to paint a picture and start that project with one main incentive; you enjoy doing it. Seeing a blank canvas take on the image of what is formed inside your imagination is a reward in itself. Seeing vivid colors pop out, taking on unique shapes and designs, with eyes wide open, you take it all in, receiving satisfaction; it just makes you smile. You're satisfied, feel fulfilled and just plain happy to use your imagination and creative skills.

The potential of an anticipated and beautiful creation that was taking up residence in your mind has now come to fruition, and you've created a completed project that initially was tucked away inside your heart's desire. It is now an accomplishment to keep and cherish forever. Do you get the idea? **God Almighty** is also wired this way, and you are this way because giftings and skills have been created in you.

So, to realize your full potential and creativity, you need to see clearly into the supernatural realm. Spiritually opened eyes are vital for seeing **God's** esoteric truths in **His Holy Word,** the **Bible**. Knowing truth comes about not so much by learning historical facts but by listening to the instruction given by **God** deep within your spirit most of all. Are you ready to perform kingly ventures? **Scripture** tells us, *"It is the glory of **God** to conceal a thing: but the honor of kings is to <u>search out a matter</u>." **(Proverbs 25:2)***

After one has heard from **God Almighty**, it takes faith to believe and heed. Simply ask for faith 'to know that you know' without ever seeing the truth with your physical eyes. After all, you can't see pain or love, but you know those exist because you sense these emotions and physical feelings. So, simply ask to have your spiritual senses, eyes and ears tuned to the spiritual realm. This is your active way of diligently seeking **God Almighty**. **Scripture** states, *"But without faith it is impossible to please **Him**: for he that cometh to **God** must believe that **He** is, and that **He** is a rewarder of them that diligently seek **Him**." (Hebrews 11:6)*

Briefly, there is a threefold reason for the creation of mankind:

א Within **God's** universal purpose for creating all on earth, there is an esoteric truth of **God Almighty** and **Holy Spirit** explained in-depth and woven throughout various chapters in this writing.

א Secondarily for the creation of mankind, it comprises a spiritual truth not widely taught, which is not only shown in the form of representation but also in a physical, parallel reality.

א Parents have a valued purpose, and their role is yet to be fully realized, an eternal destiny for their family's household.

This threefold purpose of **God** is not complicated to understand when seeing these truths with spiritually opened eyes. Beginning with the first book of **Genesis,** any child of **Father God** and **Holy Spirit** can and will receive knowledge of divine truth once seeking knowledge with their whole heart and asking for their spiritual eyes to be opened.

1 Kings 19:12... shows that **God** intends to continue speaking to **His** children who listen and heed. *"And after the earthquake a fire; but the **Lord** was not in the fire: and after the fire a still small voice."*

2 Kings 6:17... shows that our spiritual eyes can be opened to see into the supernatural realm. *"And Elisha prayed, and said, **Lord**, I pray thee, open his eyes, that he may see. And the **Lord** opened the eyes of the young man; and he saw: and, behold, the mountain was full of horses and chariots of fire round about Elisha."*

Jeremiah 33:3... shows that **God** tells us to ask for things we do not yet know of. *"Call unto **Me**, and **I** will answer thee, and show thee great and mighty things, which thou knowest not."*

Psalm 119:18… shows that we can know the deeper things of ***God's*** laws. *"Open **Thou** mine eyes, that I may behold wondrous things out of **Thy** law."*

Luke 24:31… shows us that men's eyes were supernaturally opened and still are open to supernatural truths that our minds could not comprehend otherwise. *"And their eyes were opened, and they knew **Him**; and **He** vanished out of their sight."*

Ephesians 1:18… shows that ***God*** wants to enlighten us on our purpose and inheritance. *"The eyes of your understanding being enlightened; that ye may know what is the hope of **His** calling, and what the riches of the glory of **His** inheritance in the saints,"*

In this critical time in history in which we were destined to live, we should strive to understand ***God's*** supernatural truths and to hear with spiritually tuned ears. ***God Almighty*** wants to bless and share <u>important secrets</u> with us. With us! ***(Proverbs 25:2)***

We do not want to be confused knowing ***Who*** is speaking to us, not vocally, but deep within our spirit concerning spiritual communication. The *<u>still small voice</u>'* we hear, which we should tune our spiritual listening ears to, used to be the voice of our heavenly ***Father God Almighty*** speaking out loud to mankind in the Old Testament. ***God Almighty*** came to earth and spoke directly to Adam, Noah, Abraham, Job, Moses, Joshua, etc. Since ***Christ Jesus*** came to earth, we learned that the voice of ***Holy Spirit*** speaks to us now. ***Christ Jesus*** promised that ***Holy Spirit*** would be sent to earth after ***He*** had ascended. *(**I Kings 19:11-12 / Acts 1:1-9**)*

<u>**John 16:13**</u> shows us…. *"Howbeit when **He, the Spirit** of truth, is come, **He** will guide you into all truth: for **He** shall not speak of **Himself**; but whatsoever **He** shall hear, that shall **He** speak: and **He** will shew you things to come."*

There is no Greek word for speak in the Strong's Dictionary/Translation Concordance. However, <u>guide</u>, <u>shew</u>, and <u>hear</u> bring a powerful revelation. <u>Hear</u> means…to hear, listen, pay attention, and obey. <u>Guide</u> means…to lead, instruct, explain, and guide. <u>Shew</u> means…to tell, to declare, to report.

<u>***Holy Spirit*** is present here on the earth now and will whisper into our spirit, speaking to us, giving us instruction as ***Holy Spirit*** hears from ***Father God.***</u> In this way, ***Father God***

still uses that *'still small voice'* because of three distinct reasons. This chapter explains two reasons why **God Almighty** must whisper to us. *(John 7:39)*

The first and foremost reason for **God's** *'still small voice'* is that the **Lord God Almighty** and **Holy Spirit** are all-powerful. Resident power supernaturally emits forceful energy from **God Almighty.** Simply stated, more power flows from our **Lord God Almighty** than in multiple nuclear bombs. When the **Lord God Almighty** speaks, creative, life-giving power flows out.

In our mere human form, a strong wind like a tornado or hurricane could force any able-bodied person down to the ground or send one reeling through the air. Imagine the power that is resident within the **Lord God Almighty.** We would not be able to remain alive, let alone remain standing in the presence of the fullness of **His** emanating glory and power. **Father God's Holy Spirit** must whisper to **His** children to not be overcome by **His** power and glory. We were created in **Their Image.** **Holy Spirit** talks to us, using a gentle urging and a loving voice. Power resident in **Christ Jesus** was quite evident in the Garden of Gethsemane and attested to **His** almighty power when soldiers fell backward onto the ground as **Jesus** spoke to them. *(Exodus 33:19-23 / John 18:6)*

Second and importantly, **Father God** is subtle in **His** dealings with us because of the importance of keeping under-wraps those valuable, secret matters that **He** reveals to us. Usually, this will occur over time, given in bits and pieces, like a puzzle to be resolved. As we grow and can understand the secret things of **God, He** gives us even more to understand and assimilate. **Father God** is also very patient with us. **He** waits to see if we remain interested enough and desire the things of the supernatural by getting actively involved in seeking **His** instruction for fulfilling our part in spiritual matters for a victorious life, and the increase of **His** peaceful kingdom. *(Matthew 6:9-11)*

Will we stick it out with our **Lord God Almighty** long enough to see these secret things come together and manifest in our lifetime? It took Noah many years to build an ark before seeing that first drop of rain that caused a worldwide flood; rain was unheard of. It took Abraham and Sarah many years of faith, believing throughout old age, before holding that promised child, unheard of for couples their age. Moses pronounced all ten plagues on Egypt before marching the Israelites out of slavery and into freedom. However, no one believed his report, especially not Pharaoh, that **God's** people would be free from slavery in Egypt. They refused to accept that such a phenomenal event could occur.

Joshua and Caleb waited it out for forty years in the desert, tolerating fearful unbelievers' murmurings and complaining as they wandered around before entering the Promised Land. And even when Joshua gave the phenomenal report that the wall of Jericho would be leveled, not one of the enemy armies up on that wall believed his message. But! Joshua was confident because he had listened to that *'still small voice.'* Queen Esther spent three days and nights of total fasting and prayer before her nation was saved from extinction. David, the little shepherd boy, walked up to Goliath and informed him of his soon demise. That giant didn't believe David's report either. How important is it to hear from the **Lord God Almighty** for our courage to mount up concerning any task we face? Vitally important!

It took Mary nine months of enduring ridicule, shaming, and possibly being stoned to death before our **Savior** was born. How many actually believed her report? Did they think Mary was lying so she wouldn't be killed? And **Christ Jesus** was instructed to wait patiently for thirty-three years, not raising **His** hand to heal or deliver hurting people until **His** time was right to fulfill **His** assigned destiny on this earth. Even the apostles didn't understand **Him** most of the time and struggled to believe all that **Jesus** shared with them. How long are we willing to be patient and listen? Do what others think of us matter more? Or will we be okay with the ridicule, rumors, whispering, and skepticism? *(Hebrews12:1 / Hebrews 11:13)*

Included in that group of faithful believers should be us, too. **Father God** enjoys speaking to us secretly on a supernatural level concerning many spiritual matters. Since the beginning of time, the **Lord God** created mankind for **His** good pleasure. Throughout the written **Bible,** prophets, and *'still small voice,'* **He** has informed us of **His** intentions for our universal purpose.

Here it is, **God's** favorite pleasure is to bless **Holy Spirit** by providing an excellent, living habitation for **Holy Spirit** to dwell in. The best-constructed houses, temples, and 'earthen vessels' for **Holy Spirit** to inhabit are **God's** wonderfully created, earthen clay, actively living human beings made from dust! Dust means…earth, dust, dirt, clay. *(Genesis 2:7)*

This universal purpose, being earthen vessels, is not preached in-depth at church services or taught in its entirety in Christian colleges regarding the whole truth of a person being a vessel. Nor is **God Almighty's** universal purpose for mankind impressed upon children in Sunday School classes as to why mankind has been created in the first place. Mankind's purpose is taught more along the lines of fulfilling their individualism, not in the form of tribal unity within an entire family. It is necessary to ask: Are you scholars willing to admit that we are to remain humble and ever learning? Are you a devoted student of the **Bible**? Are you willing to ask, in all humility, to be taught more of the deeper meanings of **God's Holy Word** according to **His Holy Language**? Know that this universal purpose for mankind being created is so essential for pleasing **Father God**; it cannot be said enough. And, yes, it takes faith. Yet, when you recognize the *'still small voice,'* how much faith does one need? **Christ Jesus** stated that we only need faith as a mustard seed. Paul admitted that we know in part and see through a glass darkly. He admitted to there being so much more to learn from our **Creator. (1 Corinthians 13:9-12 / Revelation 4:11)**

Our **Lord God Almighty** receives great satisfaction watching **Holy Spirit** infill **His** children with joy, peace, and love. And in so doing, mankind becomes the transparent image of **Holy Spirit** in living color. And! **Holy Spirit** is very capable of encompassing myriads of unique vessels. Created as specially designed vessels, we were originally intended to be set in places of honor in the lush Garden of Eden to beautify the Garden, with **Holy Spirit** flourishing within and flowing from out of us upon earth to refresh the world, bringing more life, love, and kindness; ever-expanding and ever-flourishing while creating more life. The best way to be our best selves is for **Holy Spirit** to be immersed within us. We were never meant to do this life alone, in our own strength. We weren't wired that way. We were created to receive supernatural help. Thus, a dissatisfied, incomplete person would have those feelings of incompleteness, uneasiness, and restlessness…you get the idea.

Relating to spiritual communication with us, it was only made possible because **Christ**

Jesus came in the flesh and died, paying the price and recompense for our selfish free will; mankind having forfeited dominion authority and our proper purpose. Mankind's self-centeredness resulted after that fruit was eaten. Like a powerful drug, that scrumptious bite caused the dwarfed reproduction of cells within our brains, our imperfect human nature. Infilled with *Holy Spirit* as was intended, we are once again restored and able to receive victorious aid, understand our purpose, and fulfill our purpose while we walk upon the earth. *(Zephaniah 3:2 / 1 John 2:2)*

And such valuable lessons about life we learn along the way! Our journey through life is almost as important as the ultimate purpose for creating us and the goals and victories we are each destined to reach. In time, we become able to handle the ultimate goal. But this is only brought about over time, learning how important it is to remain humble and not become puffed up with pride. Remember, pride was the destructive course that took down satan, Adam, and Eve. *"And be not conformed to this world, but be ye transformed by the renewing of your mind, so that you may prove what is the good and acceptable and perfect will of **God**." (Romans 12:1-2 / Proverbs 16:18 / Colossians 1:28 / Hebrews 5:13)*

In one verse, *Christ Jesus* spoke explicitly of the truth and how important it is to know the truth and not listen to the devil's lies. *"Then **Jesus** said unto those Jews who believed on **Him**, "If ye continue in **My Word**, then are ye My disciples indeed; and you shall know the truth, and the truth shall make you free." (John 8:31-32)*

CHAPTER THREE
SOME SECRETS ARE BEST KEPT SECRET

The third point regarding that *'still small voice'* inside our spirits, we human beings hear thought-voices inside our heads all day long. One would be wise to be careful what we watch and listen to. We have our own internal thought processes going on. And outside voices speak into us, causing thoughts to pass into our minds that we otherwise would not have had on our own. Be careful, child of *God,* what you see and hear.

We have *Father God* and *Holy Spirit* trying to direct us, over and above all the clamor of those other voices that race past our thought processes. What we do not need in any form is a devil's voice acting like a chameleon, confusing us as to which thought-voice we hear. We should guard all thought input by keeping our spiritual ears open and tuned to *God's* supernatural wavelength, which is our reality.

Communication with us by way of *Holy Spirit*, in secret, is vital and is absolutely our privilege to have, much like *Jesus* experienced when *He* set *Himself* apart to speak with *His* heavenly *Father,* going off to those secret places. Even if it meant *He* lost sleep, *Jesus* would make time to talk with *His Father God.* Secrets from our *Father's* lips to *Holy Spirit* and then to our spiritually tuned ears are shared this way because our *Lord God Almighty* sees all. *"He that dwelleth in the secret place of the **Most High** shall abide under the shadow of the **Almighty**." (Psalm 91:1 / 1 Cor 2:10-16)*

Our *Lord God Almighty* and *Holy Spirit* are fully aware of those sneaky, evil spirits lurking around *His* children, attempting to throw us off our destined paths. So, shush! Secrets shared by *God* are strategic meetings with the *Godhead.* These highest-level meetings should be considered valuable because those are meant to bring His kingdom to earth in completion. It is astounding to learn that we have the privilege of being *Their* hands and feet, blocking devils that roam across this earth seeking to cause havoc and chaos, especially within governmental leadership positions of entire countries. This is obvious and openly exhibited on the news, with governments wielding illegal enforcements on their nation's entire population.

Scripture shows us absolute truth and a great example in the true-life story of Samson. He eliminated an evil, pagan government during a party that officials held in honor of an idol goddess. Inside the temple of that goddess, their prisoner, Samson, was chained to pillars that held up the temple's ceiling. As they drank and performed all sorts of debauchery, Samson pulled on those pillars and literally brought the whole house down. He saved his nation from the treachery of that evil kingdom while using the power **God Almighty** had bestowed on him. This event is an excellent analogy of the authority and power in us. Samson's **God-given** strength was physical, but ours is supernatural! Do you want it?

In **Jesus'** day, evil spirits/devils roamed on earth. **Christ Jesus** called them devils. Those devils had no power over **Jesus** and greatly feared **Him**. Now, they watch to see if they can get any advantage over us, a foothold somewhere, be it our thoughts, minds, erratic emotions, or physical bodies. With our future destiny yet to be fully realized, those devils take malicious pleasure in thwarting the genuine reason for **God Almighty's** purpose in creating us. *(Matthew 10:1 / Luke 9:1 / Luke 8:30 / Luke 10:19 / Luke 11:18)*

Being deceased and discarded offspring spirits of fallen angels, who had relinquished their high positions and purposes, those wandering, lost spirits have no place to claim as their own. Their every effort is to ground mankind to earth, then drag mankind down even further with them into the pit of hell, in their restless, lost state of existence. As it has been said, 'misery loves company.' There is never enough evil performed for a devil to be appeased. *(Acts 16:16-18)*

A devil's initial tactic is to sneak in and invade a person's thoughts. Unaware human beings refuse even to acknowledge the actuality of devils. And sadly, that is precisely what those devils like; a person lying to himself about devils being active on this earth. Too, some human beings do not care to understand the difference between evil spirits and **Holy Spirit**, let alone the contrast of those subtle, inaudible thought-voices.

How do devils know humans were created as vessels to contain the **Holy Spirit?** As invisible entities, devils naturally see into the invisible spiritual realm. And so, they never would have learned to attempt to enter a person in a counterfeit form if they weren't aware of this fact. Sad to think that devils are more aware of the universal purpose for which mankind has been created than many humans! But devils realize they can only do this in an incomplete, copycat form by occupying people's minds, souls, and bodies. They know that a person's spirit is reserved for **Holy Spirit** alone.

Since devilish imps no longer have their own physical bodies to live in and express themselves through, they desperately crave a physical frame to move in and through, so they need a host. Housing itself inside a human's body is the ultimate for an invisible evil spirit, but that devil would rather the human be a receptive host. A devil's primary goal is to find an agreeable human in which to express their evil desires. Basically, a devil wants an unaware dummy, a puppet, to control. Ultimately, devils hope to neuter all human beings, thus destroying the family, by first confusing mankind as to their proper gender and then transforming humans into robots for the satanists' elites.

How does a person become a receptive vessel for a devil? That person will exhibit evil through various words or actions. When it is obvious a person is quite willing to entertain evil thoughts and perform consequent actions, that person provides an opening. Gaining that foothold, the devil spirit invades a person's body to harass them and ultimately control their thoughts and actions. It is a crushing defeat for the human being and a clandestine victory for that devil. If not dealt with, that devil will become a stronghold inside a person.

There are numerous ways this occurs: generational sinfulness; congruent, habitual sinfulness; negatively spoken words by a person of their lack of physical or emotional health; actions by a person showing willing evilness toward others; lustful or perverted words spoken by a person; greedy coveting of wealth or fame, etc. In desperation, invisible devil spirits can inhabit animals or items of furniture just to have a place to exist in. *(Mark 5:9-13)*

As mentioned, devils are subtly cunning at being cleverly disguised. Like a chameleon, a devil imp can camouflage itself, tricking a person's mind, unsettling their emotions and soul, i.e., conscience, while remaining completely invisible. This is why it is so important to listen to the right thought-voices. When a person is troubled, and there's no letup, no relief, it might be a devil causing mental or physical trauma.

If a devil finds an open door to gain a foothold, labeled sin, it will go to work influencing the person's thoughts by way of their subtle thought-voice, causing that person to dwell on negative thoughts at the very least, or hideous evil thoughts, to the point of ultimately controlling the person's thoughts. That devil then is able to live out its restless, evil scheming through that person. When a devil spirit goes to work on a person, splitting apart a triune person: spirit, soul, body, the devil can trap the person's spirit. A form of incarceration takes place. This is commonly known as a devil possessing the person, controlling their soulish mind and body, and imprisoning their spirit deep within.

Quite deviously, when a devil sneaks in, it cunningly persuades a human being to assume that he or she, alone, is thinking evil, hate-filled thoughts, contemplating performing subsequent evil actions, seemingly done in and of that person's own self-will. Though it is often a camouflaged devil, it could even be legions of devils in some cases that will cause a person to dwell on a matter, crave performing that evil action to plot it out, and finally act it out.

Those devils also cause some humans to crave a sense of evil strength and power as they subjugate others. When in control, lording over a person's will, a devil takes satisfaction in harming other humans or animals through that person, seemingly controlling whether the subjugated ones should live or die. *(Mark 5:10-20 / Mark 16:17)*

Do not trust all the thoughts that come into your mind; listen to **God** instructing you! Remember, our emotions are fickle and can cause us to err in our thinking, and devils can camouflage their thought-voices as our own. That loving, *'still small voice'* you hear is the instruction from **Father God,** given to **Holy Spirit** and shared with us. **They** want us in on important spiritual matters to actively implement resolutions. We are meant to hold power and subdue devils!

Will we listen and heed? Are we willing to strategize with the supernatural **Godhead?** Will we consider these practical matters of creativity and righting wrongs across this world enough to become part of the answer in this troubled world and bring **God's** kingdom on earth within our realm of influence? No matter our position, we each have a purpose for existing here and now. The smallest, invisible cell inside the body is intricate to other cells for the proper functioning of the whole. In **God's** eyes and creative plan, no one's purpose is less than another's. *(Romans 12:5 / Ephesians 5:30)*

Not one thing happens randomly. Everything happens with a direct conclusion and purpose already thought out in **God's** mind. **Holy Spirit** will guide us into all truth and victorious strategies. We are designed to be more than overcomers in this life because **Christ Jesus** has already overcome the father of lies. *"Nay, in all these things we are more than conquerors through* **Him** *that loved us." (Romans 8:37-39)*

As one of **Father God's** children, we should be eager to learn our **Holy Spirit's** voice speaking within our spirit. As **Jesus** stated, **He** only said or did what **His** heavenly **Father** instructed. We are privileged to have the unique ability to hear directly from our **Creator's Holy Spirit**, here with us on earth, and receive **God Almighty's** explicit instructions for our purpose and destiny throughout our lives. And we can be confident that we, too, are more than capable of being obedient, even unto death, if necessary, with **Jesus** being our perfect example of an obedient child of **God**. *(John 12:49)*

CHAPTER FOUR
GEMATRIA TRUTHS REVEALED IN HEBREW/IBREE

Supernatural *Spirit Beings*, invisible devils and unseen spiritual realms seem strange to mere mortals. And yet, aren't you curious? Shouldn't this otherworldly information make sense somehow? Wouldn't you also appreciate it being laid out in black and white? Is there a story within the story? And if so, then you certainly need to know the rest of the story. What is the bigger picture? <u>Well, the math doesn't lie!</u> The whole truth will be clearly spelled out, and the authenticity of esoteric truths will unfold before you.

The primary purpose of the Hebrew language is prophetic and creative. It speaks to things that are not, except in the mind and desire of *God*. And then, *He* enjoys creatively causing those things to come to pass. Hebrew/Ibree inspires one to look up to the heavens to spiritually view the truth of an *Almighty God* while pointing out the omnipotent presence of *God*.

Too, the Hebrew language with built-in mathematical equations shows truths in *God's Holy Word* throughout the Hebrew aleph-beth (alphabet) and corresponding number system. When studying *God's* original Hebrew language, unveiled letter-by-letter and number-by-number, we discover extraordinary spiritual truths about *God's* creation plan and ultimate *Salvation* plan. Dual and triple confirmations arise, providing answers that add up flawlessly, confirming another word or phrase relevant to that word or phrase, thus settling questions that demand answers. Plus, many parallels are presented here to ensure you can trust that these words and verses are truths.

Within the *Scriptures* alone, using mathematical equations, one can prove that *God's Holy Word* contains the only perfect language ever created. This process, likewise, reveals sound results of the *Godhead, Salvation through Christ Jesus, Holy Spirit* and even our created purpose. Like a puzzle, but going much deeper than that, a conundrum, these pieces of truth fit together. *(Zephaniah 3:9)*

It is thrilling to learn the truth about creation and that it can be proven in words and numbers within the Hebrew language. Every topic has checked out true when trying to prove it. It is like hunting for buried treasure. And then, when two or three phrases of related words on a certain topic also result in matching numbered answers/resolutions, VIOLÁ!

Then, to go to the list of definitions for each number, those also point to the truth of each equation's topic with the number resolutions being the same. Every equation is collaborated by words, definitions, and their corresponding numbers. And then, above all, to see that those are backed up with *Scriptures* on the same topic! Wow! The beautiful tapestry of this language and of creation unfolds.

Visualizing these letters and corresponding numbers helps to understand the process. There are 22 letters in the Hebrew aleph-beth: aleph, beth/veth, gimel, daleth, he, vav/wow (wow – ancient biblical Hebrew), zayin, cheth, teth, yod, kaph, lamed, mem, nun, samech, ayin, pe/fe, tsade, qof, resh, shin/sin, tav/tow (tow – ancient biblical Hebrew).

The letters in the Hebrew aleph-beth are actual words with specific meanings:

א   aleph… unity with *God,* (associated explicitly with beth)

א   beth/veth… house, tent, duality, union (associated explicitly with aleph)

א   gimel… gifts given, divinity

א   daleth… gate, open door that no man can shut, closed-door no man can open

א   he… proclamation, Hey! Behold! Look! Grace! Breath of *Holy Spirit*

א   vav/waw… number for man, connects, nails, <u>and</u>

א   zayin… number for woman, rest, seed, new life

א   cheth… new beginning of life, harmony, infinity, eternity, eternal life (birth)

א   teth… it was good, testing, comes to an end

א   yod… hand, care, consecrated, dominion, able to bring about, fire, the hand of *God*, the flame of fire (*Holy Spirit*)

א kaph… power, power to have the ability to get wealth, two hands, unity

א lamed… king, leader, teach, learn, deeper knowledge, strong tower (12th chronically listed letter is the number that stands for *God's* perfect government)

א mem…water, increases like a wave, times of testing, completion of a test

א nun… freedom, deliverance, restoration, soul, servant, signs, and miracles

א samech… shield, circle, eternity, outside of time, *Holy Spirit's* circle of eternal life

א ayin…divine perfection, good/bad choices, obedience, *Holy Spirit* opens spiritual eyes

א pe/fe… mouth, speech, words create, breakthrough, perfection

א tsade… righteousness, humble servant, deeply rooted, reaches down

א qof… bride, made royalty, priesthood, (monkey)

א resh… head, humbleness, poor in spirit

א shin/sin…light, fire, transformation/repetition, baptism of fire by *Holy Spirit*

א tav/taw… relationship with *God*

Each letter in each word is attached to a corresponding number equivalent, which is used to form these mathematical equations that are then added to find their resolutions.

Numbers also have specific meanings:

א 1~aleph, first, unity and oneness with *God* (also a defined purpose shared later)

א 2~beth/veth, union, witness (also a specified purpose shared later)

א 3~gimel, divinity, *One God* with three parts, spirit, soul, body

א 4~daleth, open door no man can shut, earth: north-east-south-west

א 5~he, Grace extended to mankind

א 6~vav/waw, man, the sixth day of creation

א 7~zayin, completed perfection, 7 days, 7 candlesticks, 7 feasts, 7 thousand years/history of mankind on earth, **Holy Spirit** carries the seven spirits of **God**

א 8~cheth, new, new beginnings

א 9~teth, fruit, mature character, finished work

א 10~yod, gentiles, kingdom, perfect order

א 20~kaph, an open hand for a blessing, cleansed

א 30~lamed, blood atonement, crushed death, the hand of **God**

א 40~mem, periods of time, new generations arise

א 50~nun, jubilee, deliverance, restoring property to family clans, freedom for a slave

א 60~samech, support, lean on

א 70~ayin, conquer, components, elements, the kingdom

א 80~pe/fe, victory in prayer

א 90~tsade, fishhook, capture, man bent over, kneeling

א 100~qof, faith, bride

א 200~resh, insufficiency or sufficiency

א 300~shin/sin, sacred number, divine perfection

א 400~tav/taw, earth in a divinely perfected period of time

Originally, only consonant letters were used in Hebrew writings. Vowel sounds were understood but never written. Jewish tribes learned their language by word of mouth. Many Jewish books and other writings still do not include vowel points.

Vowel points more recently used in Hebrew are dots and dashes known as pathach, qamets, seghol, tsere, hireq, holem, shureq, qibbuts, and shewa, with shewa short-vowel combinations. Vowel points, jots, and tittles were added hundreds of years later during 500 A.D. by Masoretic scribes to protect proper pronunciation. This was implemented so they wouldn't lose the ability to speak ancient Hebrew fluently and pass this perfect language on to subsequent generations. College language classes typically teach Hebrew using vowel points for beginners.

Mathematical equations presented here were not prepared from completed sentences. Every Hebraic word has a root, usually comprised of three letters. Key root words, with each letter and corresponding number, were used to show proofs of the **Godhead,** creation, man, woman, **Salvation**, your purpose for living, the reality of eternal life, the importance of unity, earthen vessels/temples, family tribes, etc.

Also, these keywords used here are from the Qal/Paal Paradigm, the simplest stem or root form of Hebraic words used in this text. These stem forms do not include attached pronouns, plural forms, suffixes, or prefixes. A limited Hebrew Mathematics Glossary is found at the back of this book for review. This glossary shows the breakdown of letters that make up each stem/root word used for equations developed in this book. Keywords from the glossary are used in each equation and are underlined.

The **Godhead** speaks Hebrew, and the words create prophetically from nothing, what is not, which then comes to pass. Mankind originally spoke **God's** language and will one day return to His perfect language. A remarkable truth of the perpetual value of the Hebrew language is seen when reading **Zephaniah 3:9. God Almighty** explained that one day all people will return to **His** creative and pure language. *"For then I will turn to the people a pure language, that they may all call upon the name of the Lord, to serve Him with one consent."*

Hebrew/Ibree = ayin~70 + beth~2 + resh~200 + yod~10 = 282:

(2) witness, house, tent (House of *God*)

(8) harmony, eternity

(2) union, joined

Resolution 282 in its entirety:

(200) humbleness, sufficiency

(80) mouth, speech, words create, breakthrough

(2) witness

Beginning with proof showing *God's* Hebrew language is perfect, pure, and flawless and creates:

Hebrew/Ibree ~282 + pure (flawless)~220 + *God's Bible* in Hebrew/*Word*~206 + prophetic~63 + create~203 + life~18 = **992**

dominion~209 + authority~580 + create~203 = **992**

sword~210 + truth~441 + sound~136 + witness/beth~2 + create~203 = **992**

The *Godhead* will subdue this earth with *Their* witness of truth and the Sword of the *Spirit,* which is the *Word of God.* *They* will build *Their* house in peace and bring glory to the earth and the *Household of the Lord God.* And! *They* intend for us to connect with *Their* kingdom agenda. *(Isaiah 55:10-13 / Hebrews 4:12)*

Using the meanings for the above Hebrew words, Resolution 992:

(9) bears mature fruit, love, joy, peace, longsuffering, etc.

(9) testing comes to an end, finished work

(2) witness to the truth

The whole earth is tested whether man holds to *God* their *Creator* or chooses to believe a lie. *God Almighty, El Shaddi,* searches the whole earth for those who love *Him*; complete perfection and unity will result in an eternity of family love and happiness.

Christ Jesus **is the** *Word of God Who* **dwelt among us;** *He* **creates and speaks this perfect language of Hebrew with all dominion authority:**

God's Holy <u>Word</u> (*Christ Jesus*)~206 + <u>speaks</u>~206 + <u>love</u>~285 + kingdom/dominion/perfect order/<u>yod</u>~10 + <u>creates</u>~203 = **910**

<u>speaks</u>~206 + <u>eternal</u>~144 + <u>life</u>~18 + <u>forever</u>~146 + <u>Adam/mankind</u>~45 + <u>earthen</u>~291 + <u>vessel</u>~60 = **910**

Using the meaning for *the* **Dominion Authority of** *Christ Jesus,* **Resolution 910:**

(9) testing comes to an end, finished work

(1) oneness with our *Eternal Family*

(0) eternal family circle unbroken

Again, using the completed Resolution 900, we find another matching parallel:

(900) = sufficiency~200 + divine perfection~300 + earth in a divine period (of time) ~400

(10) perfect order, kingdom

Moving on, we must also look at the promise of the possibility of us returning to our *Eternal Family.* *Salvation* is a reality in the spiritual realm. Using these two Hebrew words, *Yehowshua* and *Yeshua,* with their corresponding numbers, an amazing truth of the perfection of the Hebrew language and the *Salvation* plan is found in the following equation. *Yeshua* is the Hebrew word for *Salvation.* *Yehowshua* means… "*Yehovah Saves,*" the name of Joshua in English. The actual name for *Christ Jesus* and the word for *Salvation* are parallel and show *God's* pre-planned provision for our redemption. Jewish parents made a point to honor *God Almighty* by giving their children names referring to *God's* providence. *(John 1:1 / John 3:16)*

His name and this word, *Salvation,* emerge above all else concerning our redemption:

(*Yehowshua/Joshua*) = yod~10 + he~5 + vav~6 + shin~300 + ayin~70= **391**

(*Yeshua/Salvation*) = yod~10 + shin~300 + vav~6 + ayin~70 + he~5 = **391**

Using *Yehowshua's* name, the name above all names, Resolution 391:

(3) *Divinity, Son* is part of the *Three in One Godhead Family*

(9) testing comes to an end, finished work on the cross

(1) first *Son,* oneness with *God*

This complementary Resolution, 391, in its entirety, is amazing!

(300) sacred number and divine perfection (our *Savior)*

(90) fishhook (*Yehowshua,* fisher of men), captured mankind, kneeling in repentance

(1) oneness with *Father God*

Now, let's explore the Hebraic first word/phrase in the ***Book of Genesis***. The *Bible* introduces us to *Father God, Holy Spirit, and Christ Jesus* in a remarkable way. This word is pronounced Bar-ra-sheet, and in the English version, it reads, 'In the beginning.'

Hebrew letters that form Bar-ra-sheet are beth-resh-aleph-shin-yod-tav:

- א The aleph and beth, the first and second letters of the Hebrew aleph-beth (from which English derived the word alphabet), have a superior association, discussed at length in other chapters of this writing.

- א The beth-yod-tav are the letters in the word for house and is pronounced biyt and referred to as *House of God.*

- א The first and last letters of Hebrew aleph-beth (alphabet) are aleph and tav. Two letters in this first word of Genesis tell of the *First and Last.* *Who* had said *He*

24

is the *First and Last,* the *Beginning and End?* **Christ Jesus!**

א The first word also shows that man would have gone into the fire, denoted by the letters <u>aleph-shin</u>. The Hebrew word <u>aesh</u> means…fire.

א But! *Jesus* is shown in that first word as well, not only as the *First and Last* but too as the perfect *Sacrifice. He* would die, by *His* own <u>hand</u> offered willingly, the letter-word <u>yod</u> meaning <u>hand.</u>

א And so, *Christ Jesus* willingly chose to accept the <u>cross</u>. The <u>tav</u> stands for a <u>T</u>, also signifying a <u>cross,</u> and can mean a <u>mark</u>; once saved, we are to have the **mark** on us with the name of *God. (Matthew 27:32-38 / Revelation 3:12)*

א *Christ Jesus* is seen again in the first two letters, referring to bar-mitzvah, and <u>beth-resh,</u> two letters that form bar-son, speaking of a young Jewish boy's ceremonial acceptance of the Jewish lifestyle while following the commandments of *God.*

א Addressing <u>aleph-tav beginning and end</u>, this first word in the *Bible* addresses the fact that *God Almighty* knows <u>the end from the beginning.</u>

א All these proofs encompassed within the very first word of *Scripture* foretold that *God Almighty* is aware of all aspects of earth and *His* creation, within the <u>aleph and tav. (Isaiah 46:10)</u>

Revealed within this first compound word/phrase in the *Bible. Christ Jesus*, the *First and Last, the Beginning and End*, is the *Salvation* of the world that *God* ordained.

Also seen throughout the *Bible*, written in the Hebraic first letter <u>aleph</u> and last letter <u>tav,</u> is a specific reference to *Christ Jesus.*

<u>These two letters consistently reoccur in *Scripture* for emphasis:</u>

א The <u>aleph-tav</u> together makes a tiny, two-letter word, pronounced <u>eth</u> and has been placed within sentences to remind us of our *Savior, Christ Jesus.*

א   This two-letter word of affirmation of the *First and Last* was written in the Old Testament over 11,000 times. (There are 23,145 verses in the Old Testament, so this tiny word, <u>eth,</u> can be found at least once in every two verses.)

א   It is a small, two-letter word, <u>eth,</u> with no meaning or definition in and of itself, but is used to connect the subject of a sentence to the direct object, connecting the giver of an action to the receiver of an action. *Christ Jesus* gave *Himself* as a sacrifice in place of us to be the reparation for our punishment so we could receive freedom from the consequences of our actions.

To further elaborate on *God's* plans and purposes for creating the earth and all therein, especially *FAMILY,* mathematical equations have been prayerfully written out to provide valuable, esoteric truths taken directly from *Scripture.*

Hebraic word~numbers about the creation of mankind show astounding proof of mankind being created by *God Almighty:*

Hey! Behold! <u>he</u>~5 + ***God***~45 + ***Son***~52 + ***Word***/spoken~206 + ***Holy Spirit***~624 + <u>created</u>~203 + <u>spirit</u>~214 + <u>soul</u>~430 + <u>body</u>~430 + <u>breathed</u>~395 + <u>formed</u>~300 + <u>Adam/mankind</u>~45 + <u>dust</u>~350 + <u>image</u>~160 + <u>likeness</u>~450 + <u>blood</u>~44 + <u>life</u>~18 + <u>children</u>~94 + <u>unity</u>~22= **4,087**

<u>one</u> ***God***/aleph~1 + <u>truth</u>~441 + ***Holy Spirit***~624 + <u>formed</u>~300 + <u>dust</u>~350 + <u>mankind</u>~45 + <u>creation</u>~203 + <u>spirit</u>-being~214 + <u>soul</u>~430 + <u>body</u>~430 + <u>children</u>~94 + <u>vessel</u>~60 + <u>likeness</u>~ 450 + <u>image</u>~160 + <u>salt</u>~78 + <u>light</u>~ 207 = **4,087**

Father God and Holy Spirit and we are eternal spiritual beings. *They* formed mankind in the fleshly body to be a replica of *Their* image and likeness on this earth and to be salt and light. We were instructed by *Christ Jesus* to be salt and light as we walk through this world. *(Matthew 5:13 / John 12:36)*

Mankind is the creation of *Father God* and *Holy Spirit,* Resolution 4,087:

(4) gate open

(0) family circle

(8) beginning of physical life, eternity, eternal life, infinity

(7) new life, completed perfection

God Almighty doesn't do anything halfway!

CHAPTER FIVE
HOLY SPIRIT AND MANKIND

Looking further, in the word Adam, one discovers this name stands for a remarkable truth. Adam, <u>aleph-daleth-mem</u> pronounced awh-dawm, holds a much deeper meaning besides the meanings: man, red, ruddy or blood.

The word, Adam, stands for mankind and people of both genders. When **Scripture** refers to Adam, it relates to the man and the woman. In Hebrew, it's not proper to say a man, one man, defining Adam as the first man of all mankind.

Number values associated with the Hebraic letters in the name:

<u>Adam</u>/mankind = aleph~1 + daleth~4 + mem~40 = **45.**

Spelling out each of the Hebrew letters for *GOD*~ pronounced ~*Yahweh*:

YAHWEH = Ya = yod~10 + vav~6 + daleth~4/H = he~5 + aleph~1/We = vav~6 + aleph~1 + vav~6/H = he~5 + aleph~1 = **45.**

Resolution 45:

(4) an open door that no one can shut, the gate to Eden

(5) Hey! Behold! Grace! breath of **Holy Spirit,** the Grace of **God, Christ** died for us

How special this is to see that **God's** perfect language proves that we are made in the image and likeness of **God!** <u>Mankind adds up to **God!**</u> The **Godhead** chose to create man in **Their** image.

Resolution 45 in its entirety:

(40) new generations arise (**Father God** told mankind to be fruitful and multiply)

(5) Hey! Behold! Grace! extended to mankind!

So, we've looked at proving equations concerning the flawless Hebrew/Ibree language itself, the creation of mankind, the **Son, Jesus, Yehowshua** with the word **Yeshua/Salvation**; and the fact that Adam/mankind was indeed created in the likeness of the **Father, God, Yahweh.**

Now, **Who** is this mysteriously wonderful **Holy Spirit?** An astonishing proof is discovered in the Hebraic name for the third **Person** in the **Godhead, Holy Spirit.** **Holy Spirit's** number is seven, the fullness of perfection and completeness. Seven also carries the meaning of seeds for new life. The word **Spirit** is in the feminine gender. **Holy Spirit** contains all the attributes of the seven spirits of **God Almighty** around **His** throne: 1-the **Spirit** of the **Lord**, 2-wisdom, 3-understanding, 4-knowledge, 5-counsel, 6-power, and 7-the fear of the **Lord.** Perfection means…without defect, complete, sound, without spot, without blemish, undefiled.

Scriptures that point to a woman who is a mother of children are found in **Proverbs, Chapter 31**. And this woman is shown to have many good attributes: wisdom, knowledge, and goodness. This **Person** is the picture of a perfect **woman, wife, and mother.** Now consider the Hebraic numerical value for **Holy Spirit, Qodesh Ruach**.

Interestingly when our **Lord God Almighty** created the earth for mankind, **He** spoke, "Let there be Light!" This phrase, specifically the word light, has a very special definition. Light means…brightness, lightning, a happy attitude, relief from all trouble. Amazing that one attribute of **Holy Spirit** is light.

Equations showing the complete perfection surrounding *Holy Spirit:*

Qodosh qof~100 + daleth~4 + vav~6 + shin~300/ + /**Ruach** resh~200 + vav~6 + cheth~8 = **624**

Hey! Behold! Breath! he~5 + good~17 + **Bride**~55 + wisdom~73 + knowledge~474 = **624**

Perfect Woman, Wife, Mother as is written in *Scripture,* **Resolutions 624:**

(6) mankind is connected to the eternal

(2) unity within the house of **God**

(4) open door to the best place on earth that no man can shut, gate to the sheepfold

Resolution 624 in its entirety:

(600) = *Bride* qof~100 + divine perfection~300 + sufficiency, humbleness in *Spirit*~200

(20) opened hand for blessing, cleansed

(4) open door no man can shut, open womb to Eden

And more confirmation of the seven spirits of *God's* character with *Holy Spirit*:

Hey! Behold! he~5 + wind~214 + breathe~395 + truth~441 + *Mother*~41 + union/beth~2 + counsel~165 + understanding~67+ fear of the *Lord*~211 = **1,541**

glory~32 + light~207 + perfection~490 + truth~441 + good~17 + *Wife*~306 + *Mother*~41 + seven spirits of *God*~7 = **1,541**

Perfect Woman, Wife, Mother as is written in *Scripture*, Resolution 1541:

(1) oneness with the *Eternal Family of God Almighty*

(5) Grace extended, the breath of *Holy Spirit*

(4) open door, gate open to the womb of the Garden of Eden

(1) unity with *Godhead*

With this knowledge, we must search deeper to fully grasp the truth concerning this third *Person* of the *Godhead.* The two words, *Spirit* and *Mother,* have the Hebraic meanings… birth and life. These words also have other meanings…the immaterial part of a person, an eternal spiritual being, wind, or air.

Look at this equation concerning our *Eternal Holy Spirit Mother,* Resolution 444:

Spirit~214 + *Mother*~41 + eternal~144 + life~18 + love~13 + hand~14 (means…done by hand, custody with personal care, power, able to bring about, occupied) = **444**

Mother~41 + formed~300 + birthed~44 + *Son*~52 + seven spirits infilled~7 = **444**

The word <u>hand</u> has definite and unique meanings, in that our ***Eternal Mother*** gives eternal life by ***Her*** dominion power and personal hands-on care of ***Her*** children. With love, ***Holy Spirit*** is able to bring about children, form them and birth them and have custody over them, occupying them as well, infilling them with the seven spirits of ***God Almighty*** in ***Their*** image and likeness.

Father God and *Holy Spirit Mother* know and love *Their* children, Resolution 444:

Divinity/*gimel*~3 + <u>created</u>~203 + <u>children</u>~94 + <u>eternal</u>~144 = **444**

Father/<u>ab</u>~3 + ***Mother***~41 + ***God's Bride***/<u>qof</u>~100 + <u>formed</u>~300 = **444**

So, we see that ***Father*** and ***Mother, Eternal Spirit Beings,*** together formed life in ***His Bride's*** womb of eternity. <u>Formed</u> means…fashioned, shaped, created, forged as in a kiln by a skilled craftsman, and purposed. We genuinely are earthen vessels formed and shaped for ***God's*** good pleasure and purpose. With these complementary resolutions, we can derive the beautiful truth that mankind has been set apart above all other created things for ***God's*** good pleasure. Also shown above is another proof using the words <u>breathe</u> and <u>life</u> that ***Father God*** utilized on the sixth day of creation, creating Adam and Eve/mankind.

Creation in an abbreviated version:

<u>formed</u>~300 + <u>eternal</u>~144 = **444**

Creation in Resolution 444:

(4) elements of creation: gas, water, solid = energy/life

(4) gate open to eternity and eternal life for mankind

(4) door no man can shut, and the peaceful entrance to the Garden of Eden

Energy is the ability to move an object from one position to another. Energy never dies; it only changes. Energy can be transferred. Thus, the reality of the electromagnetic energy of the ***Eternal Godhead*** as the drawing force in our lives could also be relabeled as ***Their*** powerful magnetic force of love.

Resolution 444 in its entirety:

(400) in a relationship with *God Almighty*, a divinely perfected period of time

(40) water/womb, increasing like waves (from glory to glory), new generations arise

(4) opened door to Eden eternal

These 444 equations verify:

א We would never have been eternal spirit beings, created out of the dust of the earth, to exist in a breathing, physical body, complete with a soul/conscience, if it weren't for *Father God and Holy Spirit* together giving us supernatural eternal life encased in physical bodies.

א We are a perfect match and replica of *Them*, formulated in *Their Supernatural Spiritual Image and Likeness*.

א We are the ultimate in *God's* creation, vessels for *Holy Spirit* to indwell and do good in and through.

Surely you recall the true story of *Jesus* within Mary's womb? The archangel, Gabriel, told Mary, one of *God's* vessels of honor, the precise details of her universal purpose and specific assignment. Gabriel shared with Mary that her destiny was to carry the physical body of *Jesus* encapsulated within her womb. Gabriel further explained details of this phenomenon when he spoke of the *Eternal God Family's* presence during this momentous event; *Father God Most High, Holy Spirit (Holy Ghost) and Son Jesus* were involved in the *Salvation* plan of mankind. *"The __Holy Ghost__ shall come upon thee, and the power of the __Most High__ shall overshadow thee and therefore also that* **Holy Thing** *which shall be born of thee shall be called the __Son of God__." (Luke 1:26-35)*

Looking once more at the numerical result, 444, this also refers to soundwaves in music, a sound that is the highway or high-volume wavelengths on which our *Eternal Mother Holy Spirit* travels when entering a place. In reality, *Holy Spirit* has an electromagnetic force, flowing in an orderly, beautifully designed geometric pattern; this is that tangible, although invisible, beautiful love drawing us toward the *Eternal God Family*.

It is no coincidence that our **Eternal Mother's** name and corresponding number equivalent are 444 or that a specific musical tone or calibration has the mathematical value of 444Hz. Praise went before the Israelites whenever they went into battle, with the musicians and singers going ahead of the army. And the **Lord God** granted them victory whenever they sang, shouted, blew trumpets, worshipped **Him** with song and marched, seeing their victory in faith. **(Psalm 68)**

Truths about Holy Spirit:

א **Holy Spirit** readily responds to music, **God Almighty's** flawless musical tones, and is drawn toward musical harmony, a magnetic force. The magnetic, loving personality of **Holy Spirit** is alive and active and is that drawing force.

א 444Hz is said to be the musical calibration that David used to play on his harp when constructing psalms or songs of praise to **Father God.**

א This healing frequency is a form of energy for all life and is incorporated in sound waves within 444Hz. Incredible to visualize are water droplets that pull together, forming perfect patterns of beauty and harmony when this frequency is introduced.

א Soundwaves create beautifully organized geometrical patterns when the perfect frequency is introduced to grains of sand or water droplets.

א Sadly, the devil has its dark musical frequency full of confusion and chaos, pulling some away from **Holy Spirit's** loving, drawing force.

א All of heaven is a musical, and since we pray that **God's** kingdom will come to this earth, as it is in heaven, music must be included as part of **God's** kingdom coming into this earth.

Holy Spirit is also known to be:

א an invisible, mighty rushing wind, an active sound that permeates and overtakes this atmosphere and with an ethereal, supernatural presence

א bringing in great glory, filling the atmosphere with joy, calming peace, and healing

ℵ   overwhelming mankind under this power

Holy Spirit comes in <u>rejoicing</u> over us when the proper music is played. This is said in *Scripture* to occur when *God's Holy Spirit* comes in, skipping, leaping, spinning, dancing, singing, and shouting for joy! <u>Rejoice</u> means…to shout and sing for joy, leap, jump, spin, and dance. *(Zephaniah 3:17 / Psalm 119: 54)*

As shown in these comparative 444 mathematical solutions, we cannot have life without our *Eternal Beings* actively involved in this factual, mathematical equation called life, but most importantly, eternal <u>life</u>. The *Lord God Almighty* has genuinely given us life and our very breath. *Father God* and *Holy Spirit* always cooperate to create all life and have given us our very spirits. Thus, we are spirit beings who will live forever somewhere in eternity. We get to choose where.

<u>Let's recap, with measured power and controlled creativity, as *They* will it to be so:</u>

ℵ   The *Godhead* creates all that is living on earth.

ℵ   Our spirit beings have always lived eternally and within the *Godhead*.

ℵ   Spirit beings don't need to breathe. They are invisible, not having a physical body.

ℵ   *Father God and Holy Spirit Mother* have miraculously placed fleshly bodies of life and breath surrounding our spirit beings, actual physical flesh and bones within our earthly mothers' wombs.

ℵ   We're blessed to know that we have always been with the *Godhead*, in eternity past, and knowing that - we were - and are - and - are to come – meant to stay with the *Eternal Family of God*, actual spirit beings, our most authentic selves in our most valid eternal form.

ℵ   Also, given to mankind was the *Godhead's* answer to man's disobedience, *God's Salvation* plan.

CHAPTER SIX
YEHOWSHUA MADE RESTORATION POSSIBLE

When we see the truths presented in the Hebrew language, with equations proving these truths, we are obligated to look further into the matter of creation not continuing within the Garden of Eden. Concerning the fall of mankind, if the aforementioned holds true, what about mankind side-stepping their purpose? And, how about this crooked path mankind has been forced to take after leaving the Garden?

Is this what we are walking out? Is this why we feel uneasy and experience so much restlessness and incompleteness on this earth? And what of their consequence and the necessity for a fix? Consequences. Who could satisfy the payment needed for these consequences? We saw an inkling of this fix in the name *Yehowshua* coupled with the word *Salvation/Yeshua*.

YEHOWSHUA'S SACRIFICE made RESTORATION with the ETERNAL FAMILY possible:

YEHOWSHUA/MESSIAH~749 + *Son*~52 + man~6 + blood~44 + life~18 = **869**

Restoration was made possible by **Christ Jesus** loving **His Father's** creation of mankind, became a flesh and blood man, shed **His** blood, and offered **His** life to take the place of mankind for the just conviction and punishment of sin.

Elohim~86 + love~8 + Adam/mankind~45 + forgiveness~113 + sanctified~404 + forevermore~146 + finished~55 + government~12 = **869**

Father God Almighty accepted the finished blood sacrifice of **His** own **Son, Who,** being sent here by **His Father,** obediently gave **His** life for mankind and sanctified mankind forevermore.

Now what about our **Eternal Mother?**

Spirit Mother (in fullness of creating vessels)~444 + love~13 + household~412 = **869**

Mother Holy Spirit draws the household of **God** to their **Savior** with loyalty and love.

Adam/mankind~45 + repent~98 + free~405 + righteousness~194 + **Elohim**~86 + **Mother**~41 = **869**

Mankind repents, is made free, and becomes the righteousness of our eternal parents, **Father God** and **Mother Holy Spirit**. *(2 Corinthians 5:21)*

Salvation~391 + family~433 + mankind~45 = **869**

Salvation is for the family, restored in **God's Eternal Family**. *Ephesians 3:15*

And again, we find proof in this threefold Resolution 869:

(8) restoring family unity for eternity, new beginnings with **Eternal Family of God**

(6) man's bloodline was cleansed by **Yehowshua's** cleansing blood sacrifice, willingly taking our conviction upon **Himself** by being nailed to the cross to pay for our crimes/debts/sins and securing the forgiveness of our **Lord God Almighty**

(9) mankind's restoration to **God** by **Christ Jesus'** finished work on the cross

Resolution 869 in its entirety:

(800) = divine perfection~300 + servant/humbleness~200 + poor in **Spirit**~200 + restoration, deliverance~50 + signs and miracles~50

(60) support, lean on, outside of time, eternity

(9) testing ended, finished work on the cross

Looking to the righteous title of our *Blessed Savior, Christ Jesus*, we see one equation that emerges concerning *Salvation* in *His Name* above all names:

Jesus/Yehowshua~391 + **Christ/Messiah**~358 + deliverance~130 + captives~307 = **1,186**

YAHWEH ransomed~95 + children~94 + **Son**~52 + kingdom~135 + willing~62 **Salvation**~391 + dwell~312 + mankind~45= **1,186**

This equation points to our *Savior's Holy Name, Yehowshua:*

א *Yehowshua* is the *Person* who fully embodies *God Almighty* and *Holy Spirit.*

א *Yehowshua* is the *One Person Anointed* for the *Salvation* of all mankind.

א *Yehowshua* is the only begotten *Son* of *Father God and Holy Spirit and* holds the rightful title, *Anointed. (John 3:16)*

That equation assures us the *Godhead* pre-planned for mankind to be saved and reunited with *Them.* And the *Godhead* worked together as a family should, reuniting mankind with *Their Eternal Supernatural Family.* There was never any doubt! VICTORY is always inevitable for all who choose to return to *God's Eternal Family!* In all actuality, our victorious life has been secured for all eternity! We only need to choose to live with *Them* in eternity. The name of *Christ Jesus (Anointed-Yahweh-Saves)* encompasses an absolute truth of *Christ Jesus,* shown in the above equation, being the *Anointed One.*

And, too, it is necessary to officially prove several other points concerning *Yehowshua's* sacrifice that secured our redemption. We must see clearly that the father of lies will not be able to stake a claim on a person deemed fully exonerated of their crimes. We need to see without a shadow of a doubt that we have regained the ability to return to our eternal, spiritual dominion, and fully appointed state of being given the commission to subdue evil on this earth. We seriously need to 'know that we know' that we are part of *God's Family* and all the power that entails our position.

Christ Jesus (Yehowshua) in obedience, with the nails in His hands, and with the full measure of the flame of fire of *Holy Spirit*, has sufficiently made our deliverance and freedom possible, our jubilee, to experience our reclaimed dominion on this earth within the divinely perfected period of time, known as the one-thousand-year millennial reign of *King Yehowshua.*

One powerful equation pointing to the blood sacrifice and atonement *Christ Jesus* took upon *Himself* for us:

YAHWEH~26 + *Son*~52 + mankind~45 + *Lamb*~305 + blood~44 + slaughtered~19

+ <u>sacrificed</u>~103 + <u>crown</u>~620 + <u>thorn</u>~196 + <u>head</u>~501 + <u>pierced</u>~225 + <u>heart</u>~32 + <u>nail</u>~414 + <u>hand</u>~14 + <u>hand</u>~14 + <u>feet</u>~233 = **2,843**

YAHWEH~26 + <u>good</u>~17 + ***Son***~52 + witness/<u>beth</u>~2 + ***Word***~206 + seven spirits/<u>perfection</u>~7 + <u>faith</u>~102 + <u>obedient</u>~410 + <u>love</u>~13 + <u>joy</u>~353 + ***Bride***~55 + <u>household</u>~412 (household of ***God****)* + <u>killed</u>~317 + <u>victory</u>~781 + ***King***~90 = **2,843**

Proofs in Resolution 2,843:

(2) the witness of ***Christ Jesus***

(8) eternal life with ***God***

(4) reopened the gate to eternal life with the ***Eternal Household of God***

(3) Divinity of ***Christ Jesus***

What a wonderful picture of the loving, merciful atonement that ***Father God*** secured for us through the obedience of ***His Son, Christ Jesus***. Within the above words and corresponding numbers, we see that ***Father God and His Son*** provided our escape from hell and made the way to reunite us within ***Their*** eternal realm.

As with Abraham, who was willing to be obedient to ***God Almighty***, though it would have meant the death of his only son, ***Father God*** did what ***He*** did not require Abraham to follow through on. If a mortal man was willing to give up the most important thing he had in his life as a sacrifice to ***God***, being obedient to ***God's*** *'still small voice,'* ***God Almighty*** held ***Himself*** obligated to ***His*** promise for mankind to be redeemed, so ***God*** sacrificed ***His*** only beloved ***Son. (Genesis 22:2)***

The following equation shows the *Eternal Family's* collaborated efforts for *Their* creation and plan of redemption for mankind:

SALVATION **MESSAGE and ACCEPTANCE:**

(1) ***God***~45 + oneness/aleph~1 witness/<u>beth</u>~2 + <u>love</u>~8 + <u>begotten</u>~44 + ***Son***~52 + ***Word***~206 + ***Yeshowshua***~391 + ***Messiah***~358 + <u>perfect</u>~490 + ***Lamb***~305 + <u>sacrificed</u>~103 + <u>life</u>~18 + <u>blood</u>~44 + <u>love</u>~13 + ***Bride***~55 + ***Salvation***~391 +

birthright~227 + unity~22 + prophecy~63 = **2,838**

(2) *Yehowshua*~391 + *Messiah*~358 + crown~620 + thorns~196 + head~501 + blood~44 + nails~414 + hand~14 + feet~233 + witness/beth~2 + power~48 + finished~17 = **2,838**

(3) *Spirit Mother*~444 + unity/beth~2 + *Yehowshua*~391 + + draws~302 + Adam/mankind~45 + *Messiah*~358 + slaughtered~19 + *Salvation*~391 + good~17 + news~421 + repentance~98 + heart~32 + speak~206 + faith~102 + kingdom/dominion/perfect order/yod~10 = **2,838**

Salvation is assured and proved in Resolution 2,838:

(2) testimony of *Yehowshua* the *Anointed One*

(8) new birth, harmony, eternity

(3) *Divinity* and oneness with *God Almighty*

(8) new beginnings by way of our *Savior Christ Jesus*

The literal definition of eternal is without pause, endless, continual, infinite, timeless, and undying. Here is an accurate description of eternity: forever, imperishability, infinity, timelessness, and endlessness. You will one day go through a door into the eternal at some point. What door will you go through? It is your choice. (*Revelation 3:7*)

Yehowshua also took our pain and sorrows upon *Himself*. *He* saved and delivered us from sin's curse and its consequences. To think that we are now privileged to reenter eternity! The door has been reopened to us, and we can now go back through the gates of the Garden of Eden and eventually live in the city, New Jerusalem! And, too, we were delivered from generational curses. And so, we can expect to be healed in our physical bodies and emotional souls. Remember, *"In the beginning was the **Word**, and the **Word** was with **God**, and the **Word** was **God**." (John 1: 1 / Isaiah 53:1-12 / Revelation 3:7)*

Equation proving our deliverance from demonic oppression and physical and emotional healing are available through *Christ Jesus:*

Yehowshua~391 + *Anointed/Messiah*~358 + deliverance~130 + captive~307 + mankind~45 = **1,231**

King~90 + *Lamb*~305 + *Word*~206 + slaughtered~19 + blood~44 + sacrifice~103 + love~8 + mankind~45 + deliverance~130 + healing~281 = **1,231**

Healing and deliverance are our recovered rights. Resolution 1,231:

(1) oneness with *Father God*

(2) unity and witness

(3) spirit, soul, and body delivered and healed

(1) oneness with our *Eternal Godhead Family*

Another equation proving the completed *Salvation* experience of healing and deliverance for mankind:

Spotless Lamb~305 + rejected~101 + crown~620 + thorn~196 + bruised~25 + nails~414 + hand~14 + hand~14 + feet~233 = **1,922**

Word~206 + *Lamb*~305 + glory~32 kingdom~135 + miracle~526 + healing~281 + deliverance~130 + captive~307 = **1,922**

Note: the word bruised means…crushed, destroyed. *(Isaiah 53:10)*

Resolution 1,922:

(1) oneness with *God's Family*

(9) finished work on the cross

(2) witness of *Christ Jesus*

(2) witness of freed captives

Christ Jesus took all the blows for us. We are now privileged to experience all of the blessings that eternity offers as a free gift to us. Undeservedly, we are truthfully on the receiving end of all good things pertaining to *God.*

CHAPTER SEVEN
FATHER GOD ALMIGHTY AND HIS ETERNAL GODHEAD FAMILY

It takes three to make a thing go right. *God Almighty* **created everything. Look at the following simplified order of facts in creation:**

- ℵ   three main categories with all living things: animal/mineral/plant

- ℵ   three main primary colors from which other colors are formed: blue/yellow/red

- ℵ   three primary sun rays: ultraviolet/visible/infrared

- ℵ   three components in an atom: neutrons/electrons/protons

- ℵ   three components in a cell: membrane/nucleus/cytoplasm

- ℵ   three things up above: wind/sky/clouds

- ℵ   three stages of clouds forming thunderstorms: cumulus/mature/dissipating

- ℵ   three places in our atmosphere that exist: sky/earth/seas

- ℵ   three facts for calculating: space/time/matter

- ℵ   three forms of matter: liquids/solids/gases

- ℵ   three aspects of science: biology/physics/chemistry

- ℵ   three branches of government: executive/judicial/legislative

- ℵ   three divisions in business: CEO/management/laborers

- ℵ   threefold beings: spirit/soul/body

- ℵ   three in a family: father/mother/child

All of us living on earth have three facts in common: birth, lifetime, and death. We are threefold beings: spirit, soul, and body. *God Almighty* spoke everything into existence and everything that we have and are, involves gifts from above, even our very breath. All things have been brought about by the **Lord God Almighty, Son Jesus, and Holy Spirit.** **Their** perfection is that threefold cord that binds **They** together have allowed us to be created and ultimately included.

YAHWEH~26 + **Holy Spirit**~624 +**Anointed**~358 + **Yehowshua**~391 = **Godhead** = **1,399**

Godhead~1,399 + unity~22 + **Word**~206 + create~203 + speak~206 + life~18 = **2,054**

love~8 + joy~353 + speak~206 + unity~22 + **Word**~206 + music~510 + enter~9 + wind~214 + fire~301 + light~207 + life~18 = **2,054**

Reinforcing the truth that **Holy Spirit, Lord God Almighty's Bride/Wife** is light, love, joy, a mighty rushing wind, flames of fire, riding into a place on the soundwaves of our glorious music and worship.

The new earth restored, with the aid of Holy Spirit here with us, will be glorious!

Resolution 2,054:

(2) union with **Father God**

(0) **Eternal Family** circle, outside of time, support lean on

(5) **grace**

(4) our witness, household of our **Eternal Family**

Lord God Almighty has placed **His Word** above **His** name. In the equation below is **God's** promise for the **Salvation** of all mankind, whosoever will accept. The verse in **Psalm 138:2** tells us that **God** only speaks with integrity, honesty, and truth. It lets us know that **God Almighty** keeps **His** promises. *(Psalm 138:2 / John 1:1)*

Christ Jesus is the Word of God and the Word of God is in Christ Jesus:

Hebrew/Ibree~282 + pure~220 + **Word**~206 + wisdom~73 + dwell~312 = **1,093**

YEHOWSHUA/MESSIAH~749 + **Son**~52 + chosen~210 + white~82 = **1,093**

Resolution 1,093:

(1) oneness with **God Almighty, El Shaddi**

(0) unbroken family circle, outside of time

(9) **Christ Jesus** finished the work **Father God** instructed **Him** to accomplish

(3) **Divinity** of the **Godhead, Father, Mother, Son**

Christ Jesus spoke with power while creating the earth and all there is and with force and complete dominion authority while **He** walked on the earth. **God's** kingdom came to earth when **Christ Jesus** was here, flowing in unity with the **Godhead**. And now, **Holy Spirit** is here on earth.

Holy Spirit is the **Mother** of **Christ Jesus**. **Christ Jesus** is the **Word of God**. Hebrew is the spoken **Word** of **Their** perfect language. The following equation proves a threefold cord intertwined and binding together the **Eternal Family**.

Yehowshua is His Father's and Mother's child. All three speak Hebrew:

begotten~44 + ***Word of God/Messiah/Yehowshua***~955 + Hebrew~282 + power~48 + create~203= **1,532**

joy~353 + create~203 + speak~206 + power~48 + wind~214 + fire~301 + light~207 = **1,532** *(the infilling by* **Holy Spirit / John 3:34***)*

Our Lord God Almighty, Father of all mankind, wants us to be filled with the fullness of **His Holy Spirit**, every bit whole: spirit, soul, and body. This also includes our entire family unit. Wholeness in **God** is equated with being an earthly family united with the **Eternal Godhead Family** and is the reason **Father God** told them to be fruitful and multiply.

Unity within a family unit was the consistent theme of the **Salvation** experience in the **Book of Acts**. Entire family households turned in complete harmony to **God** and accepted

Christ Jesus as their *Savior.* Just like *Father God* wants us back in *His Family*, we have the tremendous privilege of expecting our entire family to enter into the fullness of *God's* plan for the full completion of the creation of a family. Family unity is the ultimate perfection, a loving environment on this earth, and an incredible and miraculous victory within the *Salvation* message, and we should accept no less. *(Acts, Chapters 10 and 11)*

Too, our families must honor the presence of the *Godhead* in our life. When we pray, we must believe that *They* work together to aid us in times of distress. Like the Israelites, we should always go into *His* courts with songs of praise, no matter the situations we face. The more intense the situation, the more praise and singing should come out of our mouths, shouting *God's* definitive victory.

People who have had death experiences later shared that all of heaven is filled with music. Some folks have stated that flowers, trees and even grass emit melodies resounding with lofty musical tones unheard of on earth. *Scripture* states that no one has entered heaven, but *Christ Jesus*, who came from heaven. Possibly, those with near-death experiences were given a glimpse of heaven. Or they were led to the Garden of Eden and only thought they had entered heaven because of the beauty and perfection that surrounded them? All of heaven is a musical! The perfect, ever-creative, eternal language of Hebrew/Ibree set to music must indeed be a form of exponential beauty, sound, and perfection. *Holy Spirit* is here on earth and with us now! And so, music must be played in times of worship for *Holy Spirit* to be ceremoniously transported into a place.

THY KINGDOM COME THY WILL BE DONE ON EARTH AS IT IS IN HEAVEN!

Hebrew/Ibree~282 + wisdom~73 + knowledge~474 + witness/beth~2 + prophecy~64 + righteousness~194 + life~18 + victory~781 = **1,888**

Spirit Mother~444 + dwell~312 + vessel~60 + spirit~214 + speak~206 + **Word**~206 + sing/shout~300 + forevermore~146 = **1,888**

Music, worship, and singing bring in the kingdom of *God Almighty*.

Resolution 1,888:

(1) mankind's restored oneness with our *Eternal Family*

(8) eternal realm

(8) harmony

(8) infinity

PRAISING the *GODHEAD FAMILY* with SINGING:

bride/qof~100 + sing/shout~300 + music~510 + *Word*~206 + prophetic~63 + instrument~60 + magnify~37 + *Elohim*~86 = **1,362**

We honor *God Almighty* with worship. Our *Holy Spirit Mother* brings this into a place.

Spirit Mother~444 + love~8 + breathe~395 + wind~214 + fire~301 = **1,362**

Resolution 1,362:

(1) unity with *God Almighty*

(3) *Divinity,* gifts given

(6) mankind reconnected

(2) house of *God*, our testimony, witness, manifestation as sons of *God*

With *Holy Spirit* here, we have the honor to rise from glory to glory, mounting up to higher levels of spiritual abilities, while joining together in bringing *God's* kingdom here on earth in the most excellent way. As *Christ Jesus* promised, we will do more extraordinary things than *He* had done. And too, the perfect prayer of saints is the explicit prayer that *Jesus* instructed us to say when praying to *His* heavenly *Father.* This prayer, spoken in all earnestness, causes this magnetic pulling force and the perfect alignment of true love to draw us closer to *King Yehowshua* and pulls *Him* ever closer to us here on earth. The *Lord's Prayer* is found in Chapter 21 and is set apart with mathematical equations, line-by-line. *(Luke 11:1-4 / John 14:12)*

In the *Song of Solomon*, a remarkable likeness to *Christ Jesus* and *His Bride* is portrayed by the love between King Solomon and his bride in the following Hebrew words and numbers.

SONG OF SOLOMON

Love for his bride:

lily~656 + valley~210 = **866**

wife~306 + black~508 + love~8 + blood~44 = **866**

Resolution 866:

(8) new beginning with the *Eternal Family of God*

(6) mankind restored by *Father God, Holy Spirit, and Christ Jesus'* immense love

(6) mankind black with sin, covered by the blood of *Christ Jesus*

Christ Jesus has gone to build a house for *His Bride*, and though she was black from sin, she has been washed clean with *His* blood sacrifice. Also, in the *Song of Solomon*, the word black is referencing working with her hands as a common servant or like a slave (a slave to sin), from which she has been redeemed by her *Kinsman Redeemer, Christ Jesus.*

Three words in Hebrew refer to the deep love between a husband and wife within a family unit:

1) 'ah-hav' their friendship and loyalty to one another, **(8)**

2) 'ah-ha-vah' their romantic love for each other, **(13)**

3) 'ro-yah' my darling, beloved, and object of a man's devotion. **(285)**

This threefold reference for the word love in Hebrew proves that the threefold cord of true love binds together and encompasses all forms of love: friendship, family, and even couples in love. A threefold cord cannot be easily broken.

In the following equation, it is significant that this tripled reference points to the triune cord of true love of *Father God* and *Holy Spirit* and *Their* unconditional and complete love for one another. This equation also points to the deep love and devotion of **Christ Jesus** for **His Bride**.

SONG OF SOLOMON:

friendship/<u>love</u>~8 + romantic/<u>love</u>~13 + object of a man's devotion/<u>love</u>~285 = **306**

<u>wife</u> = aleph~1 + shin~300 + he~5 = **306**

Resolution 306:

(3) unity and **Godhead** loving mankind **Their** creation

(0) love for **Their** never-ending eternal family circle

(6) mankind, the object of **God's** affection

The beautifully penned poetry in the **_Song of Solomon_** is balanced with descriptions of nature and the valley where the married couple resides during their honeymoon. And then, too, it can be compared to the ending verses in the **Bible** with the **Bride** calling to her **King** of kings to return to earth. *(Revelation 22:17)*

SONG OF SOLOMON unconditional love in body, soul, and spirit:

<u>rose</u>~548 + <u>sharon</u>~556 + <u>lily</u>~656 + <u>valley</u>~210 = **1,970**

Bride/<u>qof</u>~100 + <u>sharon</u>~556 + <u>lily</u>~656 + <u>love</u>~8 + <u>seven spirits</u>~586 + <u>prophecy</u>~64 = **1,970**

Life will be great in the new city! Resolution 1,970:

(1) unity, prophecy fulfilled, and **Godhead** reestablished in the valley of Jerusalem

(9) search for **Bride** finished

(7) perfection of fulfilled love

(0) the eternal family circle of love

It is wonderful to know that **Holy Spirit** and the **Bride** are here on earth, working together, taking back this land, and occupying territory for the coming **Kings** of kings. Are we beginning to understand more of our purpose? We must learn all we can about our birthright and take our position seriously. We need to listen to instructions from **God Almighty, Leader of His Host of angel armies.** Reading on, we will realize our place on this earth without a doubt, our reality, and our destined purpose. And thank **God**, because of **His** perfect Hebrew language, we can prove it!

Prophecy is being fulfilled, and the **Bride** and **Holy Spirit** are cleaning house for the **King** of kings. Prophecy is being fulfilled, as the seven spirits of **God** comprised within **Holy Spirit** roam this earth with the **Bride**. **God Almighty** is quite practical in **His** purpose and plan for this earth and mankind. **He** wants a clean house for **King Yehowshua** to return to. Housecleaning on this earth will make the **Bride**'s presence evident. This housecleaning process secures our reclaimed dominion authority.

HOLY SPIRIT and *Bride* say, "COME QUICKLY, LORD JESUS!"

Eternal Mother~444 + <u>wife</u>~306 + <u>faith</u>~102 = **852**

<u>seven spirits</u>~586 + <u>prophecy</u>~64 + **Qof/Bride**~100 + <u>faith</u>~102 = **852**

Holy Word Resolution 852:

(8) new life, eternity, infinity, creation ever continuing

(5) breath of **Holy Spirit** flows across the earth with new wine

(2) testimony of the **Bride** in faith

CHAPTER EIGHT
THE GODHEAD AND PARENTS AND CHILDREN

It is accepted that family is the only Governmental Institution our *Father God Almighty* has ever established on the earth. *His Eternal Family* is the perfect prototype for the creation of mankind. Though various researchers in certain nations have experimented with alternatives, no other pattern has worked well for rearing children.

Two created beings have the specified and critical task of training their offspring to stay on the straight and narrow path for their life; these two are a child's mother and father. *"My son, hear the instruction of thy father, and forsake not the law of thy mother: For they shall be an ornament of grace unto thy head, and chains about thy neck." (**Proverbs 1:8-9 / Proverbs 22:6 / Genesis 1:28**)*

Since we are *God's* creation, studying the word creation is essential. Also, the words glory and adoption are pertinent as sons of *God.* And following this line of thought, the term manifestation of the sons of *God,* it is quite interesting to discover our position as *God's* sons. These words are found in the New Testament, the book of *Romans, Chapter 8*, so the Greek Translation Dictionary was used to explain this connecting thread of evidence of our sonship. However, the Greek does refer back to Hebrew concerning the word glory. *(Romans 8:17-23)*

Glory ... glory, splendor, brilliance, excellent light that radiates from *God's* presence, associated with praise and honor, power and acts of power, words of excellence, assigning the highest status to *God* in worship. This word was referenced to the Hebrew word glory and means a stairway, winding stairs upward! One might say, going from glory to glory, onward and upward!

Actual Greek definitions per the Strong's Concordance:

Creation... a created thing, an ordinance, a governmental institution

Adoption ... sonship, greater inheritance, and honor

Manifestation ... information made known and understood by *God's* closest associates

<u>Sons</u> … terms of endearment, one of a kind

When reading the meanings of these words, **Scripture** provides information about our glorified inheritance and sonship, **God's** governmental institution with **His** closest associates, i.e., **His** family. <u>Associates:</u> one definition is…<u>teamed up together</u>. Our position of power comes from information and a clear understanding given to us by **God Almighty** with **His** '*still small voice*' for us to speak the words of excellence within the Hebrew language of **God. (Revelation 21:7)**

The only way is up! The Greek word for '<u>glory</u>' speaks to the splendor that radiates from **God Almighty's, El Shaddi,** presence…#1391 in the Greek concordance. And the Hebraic word most closely referenced from the Greek word '<u>glory</u>' speaks to a stairway winding upward…#3883 in the Hebrew concordance is '<u>lul</u>' = lamed~30 + vav~6 + lamed~30 = **66**

Comparative resolutions proving our sonship and supernatural position in *God Almighty's* governmental power within *His* kingdom:

<u>Mother</u>~41 + <u>love</u>~8 + perfect family <u>government</u> of **God**~12 = **66**

<u>Father</u>~3 + <u>prophetic</u>~63 = **66**

<u>begotten</u>~44 + <u>unity</u>~22 = **66**

<u>born</u>~54 + perfect family <u>government</u> of **God**~12 = **66 (institution of family)**

<u>blood</u>~44 + <u>unity</u>~22 = **66**

<u>life</u>~18 + <u>power</u>~48 = **66**

<u>glory</u>~32 + <u>unity</u>~22 + perfect family <u>government</u> of **God**~12 = **66**

<u>son</u> of **God**~52 + <u>hand</u> (consecrated with dominion power)~14 = **66**

<u>glory</u>~32 to <u>glory</u>~32 + (our) <u>witness</u>~2 = **66**

Resolution 66:

(6) sons of *God*, dominion power given to mankind on the sixth day of creation

(6) connecting mankind to the *Eternal Family of God Almighty*

Resolution 66 in its entirety:

(60) lean on, support, shield, *Holy Spirit's* circle of eternal life

(6) nails, sixth day of creation/mankind

So, we see in the above equations proofs that mankind was begotten in the *Eternal Womb* created by *Father God's* love and then born with the same blood DNA as eternal sons of *God Almighty*. In unity with *Them,* we have the official position of dominion power over this earth, by way of *God's* perfect governmental power, going upward from glory to glory. *(Genesis 1:28)*

Now exploring the ordinance of the marriage covenant, we will unquestionably see the governmental institution *God Almighty* ordained within the family and the unified, true love of a man and woman in their marriage covenant for building their family household.

Hebrew words and numbers show the completion of love within marriage:

love = aleph~1 + he~5 + beth~2 + he~5 = **13**

(combination of man and woman/also means…romantic love and loyalty)

love~**13** = the number of man~**6**~vav + the number of woman~**7**~zayin

This equation shows *God's eternal promise* to *His* family through *Holy Spirit:*

(breath of *Holy Spirit*) he~5 + eternal~144 + life~18 + household~412 + unity~22 = **601**

father/mankind~45 + mother~41 + son~52 + family~433 + unity~22 + love~8 = **601**

Resolution 601:

(6) mankind, earthen vessels of honor, the sixth day of creation dominion/power

(0) family circle unbroken

(1) unity in the family, oneness with **God**

Resolution 601 in its entirety:

(600) = baptism by fire~300 + divine perfection~300

(1) unity with **God**

The following equation shows the basic principle of our universal purpose within our *Eternal God Family:*

Spirit Mother~444 + light~207 + dwell~312 + earthen~291 + vessel~60 + unity~22 + glory~32= **1,368**

YAHWEH~45 + created~203 + family~433 + circle~17 + vessel~60 + image~160 + likeness~450 = **1,368**

Resolution 1,368:

(1) oneness with the Godhead

(3) soul, body created with each eternal spirit

(6) created mankind

(8) eternity with our *Father God*

We were created as vessels, family units, to fulfill our purpose and the purpose of **Holy Spirit** on this earth. Vessels akin to one another, in line together in family unity, fit together and gives evidence of the **Eternal Family** of **God**, the portrait of **Their** image and likeness. We are those who will pour out that refreshing, intoxicating new wine, causing all to be joyful and at peace. Do you genuinely want to see unity and peace prevail across this earth? This is how! Be unified with our **Eternal Mother**, here with us on earth, and work with *Her* to bring in this goodness, love, and great peace. Only by walking in unity is this abiding peace possible. An example is found in the book of *Acts,* the people listening to the apostles assumed they had become drunk early in the day, but no, this was the refreshing joy and peace that was upon them by being infilled with the power and anointing of *Holy Spirit.* **(Acts 2:1-15)**

We cannot have it both ways; self-will with self-governing independence alongside unity and peace with *God Almighty* is impossible to achieve independently. Autonomy causes turmoil, clashing with others' individuals' wills and desires. The falsehood of self-dependence allows devils to sneak in because that person has rejected the truth that he/she is subject to a *Sovereign*, not a sovereign unto oneself. Thus, that one believes their own lie, so much so that they will accept almost any of the devil's lies. Only mankind's comprehensively united agreement with the true Sovereign will bring real peace.

Father God is all about LOVE! Throughout time, *God* has stepped in and helped *His* children because of their free will acceptance of their position in the *Eternal Family. God Almighty* will also aid those lost and wandering children in the world when prayers have gone up for them. Just imagine those prayers of millions upon millions of grandmothers, prayers up there in heaven, recorded and fulfilled. *Father God* even loves obstinate children. At the judgment seat of *God,* the rebellious children will learn about the many times their *Father God* made every effort to draw them back into *His Family*. And the little ones who were not granted their life on earth after conception through abortions, or died at birth or shortly after, will one day have their opportunity to live in the thousand-year reign.

When *God Almighty* sent in the flood during Noah's day, *He* spared just four married couples in the same family clan of all those living on earth at that time. What an astonishing truth it is to learn that Noah knew Adam and was fully aware of the stories of the Garden of Eden, where all the glory of the *Godhead* had touched down on earth. And yet, out of the millions of families, only one family tribe had heard, truly listened, understood, and then heeded, and thus accepted the moral way to live by remaining obedient to *God Almighty*. Did you get that? Only one family listened to *God's* *'still small voice'* and obeyed *Him.*

The world, nations, clans, and territories had become so vile and reprobated that something had to be done. Giants roamed the land, birthed from fallen angels cohabitating with human women. **Father God** was sorry **He** created mankind in the first place. The father of lies had accomplished its worst possible delusions, perverting all mankind who lived on the devil's turf at that time. *(Genesis 6:6)*

Still, **God** searched the whole earth and found one faithful man. **He** had Noah build that ark, which took over 120 years to finish. All the while, Noah preached about **God Almighty** destroying the earth because of the rampant sin going on across the land. **God** used the power of water to cleanse the whole world of evil and wickedness. Noah warned mankind for years with the visual aide of that ark built on dry land. No rain ever fell across the earth; only dew settled on the ground. When Noah began building that ark, no one believed his report that **God Almighty** would flood the world with water. They couldn't imagine this phenomenon would occur because they had long since rejected the *'still small voice'* and chose to cling to the devil's lies. Finally, **God** shut the door to the ark after all the warnings. *(Genesis 7:16)*

God's patience had come to a halt. That flood was the type and shadow on the earth of baptism into death and resurrection into a new life. Another type and shadow displayed in the flood concerned the world itself; the seed (earth) went under, died, and rose again anew. Since then, **God Almighty** has dealt with mankind's bent toward sin in different ways. But, as with the flood, pointing to their need for death to self-will and a resurrection to a new life, this was also exemplified in the **Savior.** **Scriptures** concerning Noah show **God's** implemented plan for the **Salvation** of all mankind, whosoever will accept His plan.

There are several other parallels to be made about Noah's ark. Noah sent a dove out of the ark to test if the flood had subsided. That dove was female, and the word dove is in the feminine gender. And the dove found no resting place for her feet and returned to the ark. **Holy Spirit** has come back to this earth to be with mankind. The dove later came back with an olive branch in its mouth; the olive branch is a sign of peace. **Holy Spirit** speaks peace to us and wants to make a peaceful habitation on this earth for all mankind.

Throughout the **Bible,** this splendid example shows **God's** love for mankind in the context of family. Recorded genealogy in the **Holy Word** concerning **Jesus'** human family line in the tribe of Judah was accurately chronicled down through the ages. The importance of women and mothers within this family line was included. In **Scripture,** certain women were highlighted: Sarah, Rahab, Rebecca, Rachael, Ruth, Bathsheba, and Mary were involved in the linage of the tribe of Judah, in the family line from Abraham, Isaac, Jacob, Joseph and on down the ages to King David and which **Christ Jesus** ultimately was placed into. These women were flawed in many ways, and some were quite sinful. Yet, **God** still used them, redeeming their lives and purpose. **God Almighty** is very good at taking the seemingly hopeless person and restoring them to a new life and realizing their potential and creative purpose. *(Matthew 1:1-25)*

When the barren wife, Hannah, travailed over not being a mother, asking **God** for a child, **Father God** responded to her cries. She had made a vow to **God.** Though she desperately wanted to bless her husband with a child, she vowed to give that child back to **God** to serve **Him** all the days of his life. As parents, we should do this with our children and give them back to **God** to fulfill their purpose for being created and in **His** service wherever **He** will send them. *(1 Samuel 1: 6-7)*

The crucial truth parents must instill in their children is this: our **Lord God Almighty** created mankind *to be* the best of **His** creation, as earthen vessels meant to be the habitation for **Holy Spirit** to pour **Herself** into and also to pour out from. We genuinely are to be these picture-perfect pitchers filled up with that new and intoxicating ethereal wine!

In other words, we were created for this fundamental, universal purpose to enter into the glory that is resident within **Holy Spirit** by being inhabited by **Holy Spirit** as vessels of honor. And the perfect way is done by each family clan. In Acts, Cornelius' entire family and even his servants were saved. *(Acts 10:1-48)*

We are **God's** workmanship. Workmanship means…things that are made. Parents are to teach their children this specified purpose for being created and how **Holy Spirit** is on earth now assisting them to live this out. We are to be filled to the brim with this intoxicating, new wine of joy and love and peace that **Holy Spirit** offers, complete and entire. With individualized destinies within our family units and our dominion authority with our *Holy Spirit's* prompting, this mind-altering, mind-correcting, abiding joy will put to rest all questions and doubts. This has not been the focus of most Christian parents. In this United States of America, with our western world view, the focus is mostly on children learning survival basics for staying alive or progressing in academics to get ahead in life in this materialistic world on the national and international stage within financial systems. *(Ecclesiastes 1:14 / Acts 2:1-4 / Ephesians 2:10)*

The glorious blessing of the infilling of *Holy Spirit* was forfeited when Adam and Eve disobeyed the protective mandate of their *Lord God Almighty* and caused their fall from grace in the Garden of Eden. And for all intent and purposes, it seemed that, for mankind, this resident, shared glory of *Holy Spirit* was no longer attainable. Human beings were left to wander the earth floundering in a sea of confusion. Thankfully, we also get to share with our children that our *Lord God Almighty* had a perfect plan to rescue us. But honestly, this universal reason for all of mankind being created in the first place needs to be stressed above all else. Children should also be informed of the sad occurrence that destroyed the main objective of *God's* plan for mankind because it doesn't have to be repeated. *(Genesis 3:6-12)*

CHAPTER NINE
THE REALITY OF THE ETERNAL FAMILY VS. ERRORS IN THEOLOGY

Long-held church doctrines of three male spiritual components in the **Godhead** have been wrong assumptions, and gross errors have been taught for ages. The Trinity was also developed to thwart any discovery of the true **Godhead**. This Trinity is supposedly comprised of three male entities. Such falsehoods are written in religious books stating that the **Godhead, Father, Son,** and **Holy Spirit** have only male attributes. It has also been expressed from the pulpit that the **Godhead** comprises only male beings in origin.

The truth is that this theory of a threefold, all-male **Godhead** is entirely outside **God's** order and design in creation for mankind. **Scripture** shows that **God** had stated **He** would make mankind in **THEIR IMAGE. God Almighty** said, *"Let **US** make man in **OUR IMAGE,** and after **OUR LIKENESS..."** What is in **Scripture** was written in plurality there. Image means...likeness, portrait, image. *(Genesis 1:26-28)*

Father God Almighty has created the proper function of training up a child in the way they should go, comprised solely within the family structure. This obviously must include a female component. The theme of the mother of children/offspring flows throughout **Scripture. (Proverbs 4:3-8)**

Remember when **Christ Jesus** told **His** apostles that **He** had much to say to them, but they couldn't bear it then? This could be one matter **He** was referring to. *"I have yet many things to say unto you, but ye cannot bear them now." **(John 16:12)***

This matter that is yet to be addressed had been earlier referred to as a unique and precise connection in aleph-beth and is in the **Bible** about **Holy Spirit**. In **God's** Hebrew vernacular, this is true. Are you ready to see with spiritual eyes? Let's get into it. How can one become a child, a son, within a family unless they have a father and a mother? This profound truth concerning **Christ Jesus** is explained.

Revisited, life within the *Father God's Family* made possible by our *Mother Eternal*:

Spirit~214 + *Mother*~41 + eternal~144 + life~18 + love~13 + hand~14 (by hand and with dominion power, in the fullness of creating children/vessels set apart and occupied by *Her*) = **444**

Though esoterically hidden to the carnal man's thinking, there has never been a more decisive truth than the truth that **Holy Spirit** is indeed female in origin and structure. **The Most Precious Holy Spirit is our Eternal Mother.** **Her** virtuous qualities are clearly described in the **31st chapter of Proverbs**. These verses provide examples of a mother's life, love, creativity, and blessed gifts given to her husband and children. Those womanly attributes of a mother and wife were found worthy of being written into **Scripture.** **Father God** certainly did not use Eve as **His** example of a virtuous, godly mother figure. So, where did this example of the perfect woman, wife and mother originate from, if not from the example of our **Eternal Mother** in **God's Supernatural Eternal Family?** *(Genesis 3:4-6 / Proverbs 31:1-31)*

Holy Spirit shows **Her** character throughout **Scripture** in the context of virtuous, female characteristics. Beginning with the first book of **Genesis,** the first two letters in the Hebrew aleph-beth speak to this special connection. Again, all the children of **Father God and His Most Precious Holy Spirit** must do is simply ask. We will receive spiritually opened eyes to see this truth once asking for knowledge. *(Jeremiah 33:3 / Psalm 119:18 / Luke 24:31)*

To discover any spiritual truth, only search out the **Bible.** Unless those ideas align with **Scripture,** man's opinions do not matter. And so, we will only use the perfect Hebrew language translation of the **Scriptures** to prove **She** does exist. Following this theme of our **Eternal Mother** is the importance of proving other relevant points surrounding **Her.** Most of these points are readily accepted by established religious denominations.

Reflect on the word, mother. What purpose or function does the word mother have other than having birthed offspring? A woman is called a woman because of her gender; a mother is called a mother because she has birthed offspring. Only a mother gives birth. To be our **Eternal Mother,** we must initially come into an agreement within the Hebrew language that **Holy Spirit** had birthed **Jesus** in spirit form. Along with proving this truth, we must provide absolute proof that a complete **Eternal Family** exists. *(Ephesians 3:15)*

Consider the word dove. In Hebrew, this word consists of the yod, holem/vav, nun, he, and is pronounced Yonah (Jonah). Dove is in the feminine gender. A **Dove** lighted upon **Christ Jesus** when **Father God Almighty** spoke verbally from heaven at **His Son's** baptism in the Jordan River. **God Almighty** was there, **Holy Spirit** was there, and **Christ Jesus** was there at **His** baptism. This **Dove** attests to **Holy Spirit** as feminine. In celebrating **His** baptism, the entire **Eternal Family of God** was there when **Christ Jesus** was baptized into **His** commission and received the fullness of **Holy Spirit** without measure. *(Matthew 3:16)*

Now concerning Eve, whom Adam named as the mother of all living, it is understood that Eve was the first woman to conceive children here on earth with physical bodily forms. So yes, she was said to be the mother of all living, physically embodied human beings. However, their spirits were previously created within the forever, never-ending circle of eternity by **Father God Almighty** and **His Most Precious Holy Spirit Wife,** our **Eternal Mother.** **Father God** lovingly placed each of our spirits into our physical bodies, and **Holy Spirit** breathed eternal life into our spirits and bodies. Certainly, Eve did not do this.

To be a spirit being, we had to have been born by our **Spirit Being Mother.** Remember, only a mother gives birth. **Spirit** is born of **Spirit,** and flesh is born of flesh. *(John 3:6)*

We were born of and by our **Holy Spirit Mother.** However, born is a word that, on the surface, does not perfectly speak to the complete truth about us remaining in the presence of our **Eternal Mother.** To say we were genetically born spirit beings of **Holy Spirit** is to say that since our **Holy Spirit** was, is, and always will be, so too, we spirit beings have always been since our **Eternal Mother** has always existed.

We were in heaven, eternal spirits existing before we were born in human flesh. We have always been outside of time and space. Our spiritual births never started or began in time and space but have unceasingly resided within **Holy Spirit Mother's** womb of protection. We could liken this truth to being within the womb of the morning of creation, in the Garden of Eden. All were protected there, and all needs were provided for mankind like within a mother's womb. **Scripture** reads that the **Spirit** <u>hovered</u> over the earth. In **Genesis** and Hebrew, <u>hovered</u> is in the feminine gender and means…like a hen hovers over her chicks. *(Genesis 1:2)*

Consider the truth that **God Almighty** is omnipresent, everywhere, all the time. No one can hide from **God Almighty**. **God** is even inside the womb, which was shown to be true in **Scripture** when Gabriel visited Mary. The **Godhead** was said to be inside her womb. **Father God and Holy Spirit** are involved in **Their** spirit being children gaining a flesh body like was with **Christ Jesus. (Luke 1:35)**

David penned in **Psalms** that **God** would be there even if he went into Sheol. (Sheol in Hebrew means...down to the grave.) So, it is true that **God** is everywhere, even within the womb. Could there be much more to the creation of life and the pureness of holy intercourse than we have ever dared to imagine? When one considers how the father of lies has perverted sexual intercourse and turned marital love into fornication and lust, it is reasonable to assume that much more to experience about love and perfection in the act of conception was reserved in the Garden. *(Psalm 139:8)*

CHAPTER TEN
ALWAYS AND FOREVER ETERNAL SPIRITS

Jesus stated that <u>we must be born again of the *Spirit*</u> to reenter the kingdom of heaven. We are a spirit being and have been given a soul/conscience, and we also live in a physically constructed frame or shell called a body. <u>Our spirit is eternal.</u> *(John 3: 5-6)*

To reiterate, the truth is that we were born in *Their Eternal Family*'s supernatural, spiritual realm, outside of time and space. Eternal life was only accomplished by our *Holy Spirit Eternal Mother* to be a spirit being who will live forever. *(1 John 5:11)*

We came to earth in the likeness of sinful flesh within the womb of our physical earthly mother, who has a fallen, sinful nature. And so, we must be born again in the *Spirit*. <u>Born again in the *Spirit* refers to initially being born in the *Spirit*.</u> *Jesus* was not referencing being born in the flesh initially but then needing to be born in the *Spirit* in the flesh again. *Jesus* meant and said reborn in the *Spirit*; that is born again a second time in the *Spirit*. <u>Eternal</u> means…everlasting and is akin to sharing a characteristic of the *Eternal God.* *(John 3:6)*

Indeed, we were born once in heaven. Aside from time and space, *Holy Spirit* is our *Eternal Spirit Mother*. Our fallen human nature became part of us when we were born in the flesh in our physical mother's womb. So, we now must be willing to return once again and accept our position within our *Eternal Family*.

In the book of *Titus,* Paul assures us that we are saved according to *His* mercy by the <u>washing of regeneration</u> and <u>renewing by *Holy Spirit*.</u> These two words, <u>regeneration</u> and <u>renewing,</u> speak to our birth in spirit form as a spirit being by our *Holy Spirit Mother* in heaven. Then we were born in the flesh, completing our triune being. Remember, *God Almighty* does all creating in sets of three. We must now start over to get back to where we were outside of time and space, an eternal spiritual being. In this transformation, are we starting over in another fleshly body as a different physical being without a physical, fallen nature? Nope. It is required that we revert to the eternal position we once held, and thankfully, we have been permitted to receive once again for whosoever will accept this gift of eternal life. Remember, the *Scriptures* read that flesh and blood cannot enter into heaven, and corruption cannot inherit incorruption. The corruption must put on incorruption, and the mortal must put on the immortal. <u>Washing</u> means…bath, wash. <u>Regeneration</u> means…rebirth and restoration. <u>Renewing</u> means…renewal, <u>start over.</u> *(1 Corinthians 15:49-55 / Titus 3:5)*

As **Father God** told Jeremiah*, He* knew us before we were placed in a physical, fleshly womb in bodily form. Each person existed previously as a spirit being. Sin entered mankind, polluting us, so there was no longer a place for the **Most Precious Holy Spirit** to reside within **God's** created vessels.

<u>Mankind's spirits were then literally up for grabs by any spirit we would choose to accept and let in. And too, being on the devil's turf outside the Garden, evil spirits could invade souls and minds in stealth ways.</u>

As clarified in previous equations, being reborn of our **Holy Spirit Mother** once again, this reality was made possible only after **Jesus** paid for our fallen sin nature, so our spirits would have the opportunity to be cleansed to contain the fullness of our **Holy Spirit Eternal Mother.** Sad to consider, Adam and Eve had lost the infilled glory of **Holy Spirit** when they disobeyed and subsequently discovered they were naked and exposed. *(Jeremiah 1:5 / John 3:5-6)*

Reading this **Scripture** verse, we see this truth that we, too, have always been in spirit form, like **Jesus**, before we came to earth in the flesh. *"Before I formed thee in the belly, I knew thee..."* *(Jeremiah 1:5)*

Though **Father God** shared this truth with the prophet, Jeremiah, he did not remember being in **God's Eternal Family** before his proper time came to live in the flesh on earth. All mankind must now accept this gracious blessing from **Christ Jesus** to start over and be as we were before. And know that, during the millennial reign, **God Almighty** has made provision for those resurrected when **Christ Jesus** returns to know **Him**, those who had never heard these truths before their death.

When **Christ Jesus** walked this earth, **He** said they believed because they saw **Him** in person. **Jesus** promised that those who receive **His** blessing of renewal with **God's Eternal**

Family in faith are doubly blessed for believing in His sacrifice though not having witnessed *Him* perform miracles with their own eyes. Because of open rebellion done by Adam and Eve forfeiting that precious glory, we must again use our free will to accept these truths. *(John 20:29)*

Like Jeremiah, *Jesus* had no actual memories of this truth about existing in heaven before entering Mary's womb. Only by faith, *He* believed and spoke of this truth openly because *He* fully trusted in *His Father's* '*still small voice*' when *He* was taught in secret by *His Father* that *He, Jesus,* is the *Creator* of all on earth. *(John 15:15)*

Only by faith in *God* did *Christ Jesus* believe *His Father's* instruction that *He* must die to save mankind. *Christ Jesus* taught that a seed must go into the ground and die, thus granting life to other seeds and producing more seeds because of the one seed's death. *Jesus* honored *His Father's* instruction by being obedient to die on the cross for our sins. After being taught throughout *His* childhood, as *He* grew in wisdom, stature, and favor with *God* and man, receiving knowledge in secret of *His* purpose on earth, *Christ Jesus* understood that *He* is the *Savior of the world. Jesus* said all *He* said and did all *He* did, in faith, because *He* knew *His Father's* voice. *(Luke 2:52 / John 10:14-18)*

Christ Jesus was our perfect example. We, too, must die to our carnal, fleshly nature and be reborn. Once reborn in the *Spirit,* we're living vessels, spirit, soul, and body, containing our *Holy Spirit Mother* in our supernaturally transformed/transfigured physical bodies. Christ Jesus exhibited this wonderful truth while walking on this earth. *(Matthew 17:1-8 / Mark 9:1-8 / Luke 9:28-36 / 2 Peter 1: 16-18)*

CHAPTER ELEVEN
CONCEIVED WITHIN THE ETERNAL REALM

Eve was also one of **Holy Spirit's** designed vessels. The glory of our **Father's Holy Spirit** was all over, within, and throughout Eve before her fall from grace. The glory that was upon Adam and Eve was not their own resident glory within themselves. This glory was imparted to them by the infilling of the **Most Precious Holy Spirit**, their **Eternal Mother**, **Who** had breathed human life into their physical bodies and placed their forever spirit-being-selves inside. *(2 Timothy 2:21)*

God Almighty clothes animals in unique ways with fur, feathers, and scales. Mankind was clothed, too, inside the Garden of Eden. The only clothing needed initially was the glory of **Holy Spirit** covering, as vessels shining in and throughout by being infilled with **Her** presence. Man was once wholly protected; pure, modestly, and gloriously shining, clothed with the **Most Precious Holy Spirit's** breath on us and **Her** covering of Grace and Glory! A good mother makes garments for her children, as in **Proverbs 31**. <u>Vessels of honor!</u> We are able to contain this glory once again! And we will be clothed, enrobed in that glory. Thus, the term white robes of fine linen at the wedding feast. John could only speak to what he understood when he envisioned those saints in glistening white apparel. *(Genesis 3:21 / Revelation 19:8)*

Eve and Adam's nakedness was the resulting visible proof that **Holy Spirit's** glory had departed. Adam saw his naked wife and wondered at her, so he also tasted the fruit. Could he have been curious what he would look like naked, too? Lust and vanity had entered the pureness of the Garden of Eden. Animal skins were then provided for them. **God** had to kill animals meant to live forever in the Garden. An animal never sees itself naked; it is dead if it is naked. Adam and Eve had bare skin because of their disobedience; they would eventually die. It took Adam close to one thousand years to die. "…that one day is with the Lord as a thousand years and a thousand years as one day." *(2 Peter 3:8)*

Because of man's sin, **God** was forced to make other accommodations for their exposed naked bodies. The blood of an animal was shed because of their sin. This forced a sacrifice and foreshadowed the atonement for their sins and subsequent animal sacrifices required in the temple by Jewish priests. All of that was done to point to a pure sacrifice yet to come, to pay the debt for our sins once and for all, our full redemption by the precious shed blood of the *Spotless Lamb. (Genesis 3:8-11)*

And yet, the half has not been told of all the possible aspects of the Garden of Eden. It is entirely plausible that many men and women were created in the Garden of Eden. Though not known for sure, the word Adam, referring to both man and woman, could point to many human vessels in the Garden before the fall of mankind. One verse in *Scripture* that leads one to think along these lines is that *God Almighty* said that women would have pain in childbirth outside the gates of Eden. Could it be that many other children were born, and the women, Eve included, had children in the Garden, experiencing no discomfort during childbirth? One day we will understand all that had transpired in the Garden of Eden. *(Genesis 3:16 / Genesis 5:4)*

Genesis 3:14-15 refer to *Jesus* coming to earth in the flesh; *God Almighty* said *He* would put enmity between the serpent's seed and the <u>seed</u> developed within the <u>woman</u>. *God* spoke of *One* definite seed in that verse of *Scripture*, *Christ Jesus*. This is widely accepted as truth. This woman spoken of in these verses was not Eve, not Mary, not any other human woman who has lived on earth. This woman, *Mother of Her Seed, Jesus,* is the *Most Precious Holy Spirit, Eternal Mother of all Father God's eternal spiritual beings.* <u>Seed</u> means…semen, seed, and propagates offspring. A man cannot, in and of himself, produce a child from his semen alone. What good is a man's seed if there is no woman to be the mother, the Garden, to cultivate his seed? <u>Woman</u> means…woman, wife, and to marry. *Holy Spirit* is this woman and wife married to our *Father God Almighty*. And this leads to the question, what truths do we still not know about the Garden of Eden? *(Genesis 3:14-15 / Revelation 12:1-17)*

Why would those Hebraic words <u>seed</u> and <u>woman</u> be written in those verses, with their meanings: semen, offspring, propagates, life, wife, marry, if those words aren't referring to the vitally important truth of our *Eternal Holy Spirit Mother?* It is good to recall that in Hebrew, words take on either a feminine gender or a masculine gender, which determines the type of suffix endings for words. *EL* means…*God. Elohim* means…*God* and is written in the masculine gender. The word *Spirit, Ruach,* takes the feminine gender.

Again, we were each created outside of time in spirit form. This is difficult to explain, let alone comprehend, but consider the circle and the family circle. There is no ending with a circle. And look back to the chart for the letter, <u>samech</u>, it is a circle and stands for eternal life and family. We always were with **God's Spirit Family,** this **Eternal Family** circle. And since **God** always was and we are **His** spirit being children, we always were and always will be. As stated before, we will live for all eternity somewhere, and we get to choose where.

Most religious sects believe and teach that we are spirit beings and will live forever somewhere in eternity. Religious teachers should consider what constitutes eternity, eternal or immortality. A spirit being is infinite, which means that spirit is immortal. And so, thinking it through logically, it follows that a spirit being always has been a reality. Time holds no station in eternity. Immortal is everlasting, existing before time begins and after time ultimately ends. Time has a start, goes along a linear line from one point to the other, and then has an end; this is precisely how we keep track of time.

It is a fact; eternity is now and has always been a reality. **Father God, Holy Spirit,** and **Christ Jesus** live in this realm of eternity. We, too, are spirit beings and have always lived forever, before time began, and will continue to be forever. Like a circle with no beginning and no end, we live within the family circle of the **Supernatural Spiritual Godhead Family.** We human beings are spiritual beings, in a fleshly body, with a soul, at this time and season in our lives while here on earth: spirit, soul and body. And even as we live and are active within a physical body now, we must accept the truth of the fullness of always having existed as eternal spirit beings.

And at the appointed time for our destined purpose in earth's history, we were each allowed to be born in the flesh to earthly parents, in the image and likeness of the **Godhead Family**, born into a family. Because of our sinful, fallen nature, polluted by self-will, we could no longer remain in the presence of an all-powerful **Godhead Family.** It is imperative that we be <u>cleansed</u> and reborn, born again in and of our **Mother Holy Spirit.** Even the priest, Nicodemus, had difficulty understanding this vital truth when he secretly snuck in through the night to converse with **Jesus.** <u>Cleansed</u> means…purified, cleansed, to make clean, purged, eliminated, removed, disposed of, ejected, crushed. **(John 3:1-21)**

How are we cleansed? Who cleans the house? The dutiful wife/mother does the housecleaning, and a good mother teaches her children how to clean the house. As a devoted *Son, Jesus* was instructed to cleanse the temple, forcing out corrupt money changers when *His* ministry began. Later, when *Jesus* was about to end *His* time on earth, *He* cleansed the temple of its corruption once more. *(John 2:13-25)*

So too, *Jesus* initially cleanses us with *His* blood, making us white as snow, and we are then given a measure of *Mother Holy Spirit*. *Jesus* was given *His Mother Holy Spirit* without measure. The *Dove* lighted upon *Jesus*, proving *He* was infilled with *Holy Spirit*. *Jesus* is our example of every blessing *Father God* has available for us. We simply need to be instructed as to our universal purpose and secondary specific purpose, living by faith and walking in the power of *Holy Spirit*. And we can be assured that we have this privilege of supernatural power, the sword of the *Spirit,* which is the *Word of God.* This word Sword is in the feminine gender, so we are to speak boldly and wield the Sword/*Word of God*, which creates good or puts down the enemies of *God Almighty. (Matthew 16:19 / Matthew 18:18 / Ephesians 6:17)*

Here is the proof of our authoritative power provided by our *Eternal God Family*:

YAHWEH~26 + Spirit~214 + sword (of the *Spirit*)~210 + Yehowshua~391 + power~48 + dominion~209 + authority~580 + earth~291 + dwell~312 + children~94 + birthright~227 = **2,602**

Mankind~45 + willing~62 + obedient~410 + eternal~144 + vessel~60 + light~207 + speak~206 + faith~102 + pure~220 + Word~206 + wisdom~73 + build~57 + kingdom~135 + earth~291 + peace~376 + love~8 = **2, 602**

Progressing more profoundly into the supernatural and spiritual things of *God,* understand that *Holy Spirit* graciously came back here to earth, willingly to remain on this fallen earth and outside of the wondrous Garden of Eden, so *She* can fill us up wholly and cleanse us deep within, thoroughly immersing us with *Her* new wine so that nothing else can get into us except *Her* goodness, bringing true peace to this world.

Our *Mother* cleans us up, fills us up, and consequently, any residue of trash left in us overflows out and away, i.e., any devils clinging to our soulish selves. We look to **Scripture** to see *Her* wonderful spiritual attributes/fruit that *She* places inside of each of us. *(Matthew 21:12 / John 2:11-12 / John 3:34 / Galatians 5:22-23)*

CHAPTER TWELVE
THE ETERNAL FAMILY PORTRAIT

We are encouraged in **Scripture** to ask for wisdom to understand all truth. In the **Book of Proverbs, Chapter 31,** Wisdom is spoken of as a **Mother** and a **Woman**. And the word wisdom in Hebrew is actually in the feminine gender. This word points us directly to our **Most Precious Holy Spirit Mother** and **Her** supernatural attributes given as gifts to **Her** children. Wisdom means…essential, supreme condition, fundamental, indispensable. *(Proverbs 4:5-6 / Proverbs 31:1-31 / James 3:17 / 1 Corinthians 12:4-10)*

As with several other truths, this bears repeating; it has long been established that family is the only governmental institution our **Father God Almighty** instituted. **God Almighty** did not begin this earth's organized, working functions by appointing a president, king, or an administrative board with a CEO. As a matter of fact, **God Almighty** opposed mankind to having an earthly king to rule them. **He** knew a mortal man would take advantage of his subjects with egotistical pride. *(1 Samuel 8:10-17)*

Instead of man's system of institutions, **God Almighty** began **His** government by instituting family; a husband and a wife, having been appointed with dominion authority over all else on earth. **He** instructed them to multiply and subdue the earth. *"And **God** blessed them, and **God** said to them, Be fruitful, and multiply, and replenish the earth and subdue it"* Subdue means…to bring all else under their control. *(Genesis 1:26-28)*

Notice in verse 26 **God** said that mankind was created in **THEIR IMAGE**, male and female. *"In the image of **God**, created **He him**, male and female, created **He** them."* Right there is shown the **female** component in the creation of mankind. No one disputes the truth that **God Almighty** created males and females and told them to multiply. However, most deny that **God Almighty** created females in **His Glorious Wife's Image**, which is odd since it is written in **Scripture**. Multiply means…to rear offspring. *(Genesis 1:28)*

Unsurprisingly, **Holy Spirit** holds a very active part in creation in the first verses of **Scripture**. *"And the earth was without form, and void: and darkness was upon the face of the deep. And the **Spirit of God** moved upon the face of the waters."* Spirit means…immaterial part of a person and to breathe upon. Moved upon means…to tremble, shake, flutter, to hover

over. *(Genesis 1:2)*

David sang of this truth, as well. *"**Thy** people shall be willing in the day of **Thy** power, in the beauties of holiness from the womb of the morning: thou hast the dew of **Thy** youth."* The word <u>beauties</u> means…so beautiful as to instill awe (in *Her* admirers). <u>Holiness</u> means…the sacred thing set apart. <u>Womb</u> means…a mother and any female giving birth with an open womb, able to conceive. <u>Dew</u> means…a youthful childhood. <u>Morning</u> means…dawn, light, and early morning. *(Psalm 110:3)*

David sang of the reality of **Christ** being born in spirit form in the early morning of creation, before all else was created, within **God's** timeline for creation. *"…one day is with the **Lord** as a thousand years, and a thousand years as one day." (2 **Peter** 3:8)*

The purpose of sharing this **Psalm** is to point out that **Christ Jesus** was already born in spirit form. And for **Him** to be previously existing and in **His** youthful childhood, remaining in the proper order of **God's** creative mandate for how a child, in spirit form, is to be, **Jesus** had to have been created from and by a woman, **His Mother,** and it also follows of and by **His Father.** The **Mother and Father** of all life are the original life-givers of life. This **Mother** is all light and is the spark of fire that jumpstarts all life while placing their eternal spirit and breath of physical life within **Her** children.

It has been discovered, through modern technology, that during the moment of conception, a spark of light bursts forth and brightly shines within the mother's womb. This is the spark of life that only our **Holy Spirit Mother** can give to **Her** children. *"In **Him** was <u>life</u>, and the <u>life</u> was the **Light** of men."* *"**He** will baptize you with **Holy Spirit** and <u>fire</u>." (John 1:4 / Matthew 3:11)*

"And suddenly, there came a sound from heaven of a mighty rushing <u>wind,</u> and it filled the house where they were sitting. And there appeared unto them cloven tongues like as of <u>fire,</u> and it sat upon each of them." <u>Life</u> means…physical, spiritual, and eternal life. <u>Light</u> means…daylight, fire, and firelight. <u>Wind</u> means…breath, wind. **Ruach (Spirit)** in Hebrew means…wind, an invisible force, a spirit being. <u>Fire</u> means…fire, flames. *(Luke 3:16 / Acts 2:1-4)*

As read in **Scripture**, it is easy for us to accept the truth that **God Almighty is Christ Jesus'**

Father. So, *Jesus, Their Son,* had to have been previously born/created for *God to be His Father. His Mother,* the *Most Precious Holy Spirit,* conceived *Jesus* and birthed *Him,* within the eternal circle of eternity in spirit form, before creating the earth.

Jesus then worked with *His Father* and created all on earth, including the earth itself, planning for a suitable habitation for *His Mother, Who* would one day search this world for *His Bride.* As pre-planned, *Jesus* was then born/created in the flesh, being sent here to settle the debt mankind owed because of our sinful nature, with *His* pure blood sacrifice paying for the sins of all mankind. *"And there came a **Voice** out of the cloud, saying, This is **My** beloved **Son:** hear **Him**." (John 1:3 / Luke 9:35)*

This *Family Portrait* is the *Eternal First Family,* existing in the eternal *Family Circle* outside of time; *Father God, Son Jesus, and Most Precious Holy Spirit Mother.* And likewise, we are in spirit form, whom *God* knew before we were born in a fleshly, physical body shell, earthen vessel.

Father God **instructed *Jesus* to create the earth:**

- ℵ This included the Garden of Eden. *God Almighty* took great pleasure in coming from heaven to earth to walk and talk with mankind in the Garden of Eden.

- ℵ Void of any corruption, filled with *Holy Spirit,* those created spirit beings were vessels of honor in the likeness and image of *Holy Spirit.*

- ℵ Original, created beings were the perfect vessels for *Holy Spirit* to have *Her* presence in and through because *God* never creates the imperfect.

- ℵ Adam and Eve/mankind were never to experience the knowledge of the difference between good and evil, not only so they'd never know the pain of evil, but so they'd remain pure, holy, spotless, and sanctified by the invisible *Holy Spirit. (1 Corinthians 6:19 / 1 Peter 1:2)*

The *Most Precious Holy Spirit* is so amazingly glorious! And we are wonderfully made, vessels created to contain *Her* gloriousness! *She* is worthy of having much more than a mere brick-and-mortar house in which to live and move throughout and have *Her* way.

Scripture also states that we are *God's* possessions. *(Acts 7:48 / 1 Peter 2:9)*

It would be advisable to note the vast difference between the glorious and the profane. There are objects of idol worship the devil has counterfeited that have been brick and mortar statues or pagan buildings called temples. And with corrupt scientists working with AI these days, the devil and its evil human subjects have stepped up its game with holograms, trans-human experiments, and robotics. *(Judges 16:23 / 1 Samuel 5:1-8)*

Concerning temples, an analogy of *God's* institution of marriage has the truth shown in the Jewish culture, where the bridegroom goes away and builds a house for his bride. *Father God* had done so for *His Bride* when *He* instructed *His Son* to create the world and all that is in it. Solomon did much the same for *God* by building a temple and gardens. The Queen of Sheba heard of its beauty and traveled many miles to view the spectacle. The queen said that the half had not been told about the luxuriousness of Solomon's temples and gardens. Much more splendor has *Father God Almighty* placed in *His* creation, with unusual plants, animals, mountains, rivers, lakes, and oceans! And then, too, this Garden of Eden is still tucked away somewhere on this earth, guarded by *God's* cherubim. *(Genesis 3:24)*

Christ Jesus later promised *He* was going away to build a residence for *His Bride*. It is not just an allegory. It is a fact. *God Almighty* is very practical and has expertly used *His* Hebrew language with mathematical truths, having laid out plans to prove everything *He* does when we set ourselves apart to search it out. *God Almighty* only deals in reality and possesses the highest efficiency in all applications. When *God* speaks, it makes sense.

Taking *Scripture* verses and following only the reality of truth and sensibility, great similes point to our relationship with *Christ Jesus*:

- **The church as *Jesus' Bride*;** in reality, there is no way the church can simultaneously be the church and the **Bride**. *Jesus* would never marry men or multiple women. It would go against *Scripture*. *(Ephesians 5:25-27)*

- **New Jerusalem City is adorned as a bride;** in reality, there is no way that the New Jerusalem City, not yet descended out of heaven, would be a bride for a physical man.   Everything **Christ Jesus** said when **He** walked on earth is substantiated and makes sense.   How could a city be a bride, and how could a bride be both men and women?   Could a bride be multiple people, men, and women, and too, how could a bride be a massive group of people and a new city at the same time? *(Revelation 21:2)*

א **As the guests in white robes at the Wedding Feast of the _Lamb_**; in reality, there is no way the church can be guests at the wedding and also be the **Bride** at the same time.   There is the **Bride**, and the church comprises the guests attending the wedding feast. *(Revelation 19: 8)*

א **As five of ten virgins, with oil lamps lit, with the _Bride_ awaiting the _Bridegroom;_** there is no way that the five wise virgins can be the bridal party hidden away with the **Bride** and also be the **Bride** at the same time.   But yes, we will be hidden away.   *"For the **Lord** loveth judgment, and forsaketh not **His** saints; they are preserved for ever: but the seed of the wicked shall be cut off." (Psalm 37:28 / Revelations 3:10 / Revelation 12:1-17)*

These verses in allegory form are woven all through the **Bible.   Father God** even spoke of Israel as **His** wayward **Bride** in an allegory.   However, this was an example of an unfaithful bride.   All **Scripture** is consistent and points to **God Almighty's** order for **His** creation and the method **He** has originally laid out for marriage and family. *(Zephaniah 3:2 / Acts 7:48-51 / Acts 17: 28 / John 14:3)*

CHAPTER THIRTEEN
THE GOD FAMILY AND THE GARDEN OF EDEN

The Garden of Eden has been referred to in previous chapters. Continuing with proofs and going back to the beginning of creation, when mankind fell and was no longer found worthy to contain the glory of *Holy Spirit of God* living inside them, the *Most Precious Holy Spirit Mother's* glory was forced to depart from the polluted earthly vessels. That was when they realized their nakedness and shame infiltrated their souls.

Eating the forbidden fruit caused Adam's and Eve's minds or brains to be altered, and a prohibited and foreign enlightenment invaded their minds with the knowledge that evil is a reality in this world. Their brains were short-circuited negatively, gaining knowledge of the vast difference between good and evil. It was an overload of information that they never were meant to have to respond to.

Our *Lord God Almighty* didn't plan for mankind to be stupidly naïve in not knowing evil; He only wanted to protect us from all forms of corruption, such as dwelling on sin within our minds. Evil is equated with sin. After learning about the evils of lust, when Adam and Eve heard *God* walking in the Garden and calling for them, they were naturally embarrassed. They experienced feelings of shame at having disobeyed, and the thought of being discovered naked was humiliating. They were no longer engulfed under the protection or robed in the sheltered glory of their supernatural *Holy Spirit Eternal Mother. (Genesis 3:7)*

When *Scripture* states that their eyes were opened, that verse doesn't mean they were blind before. Their spiritual intelligence had been securely protected. But then, they were enlightened to the reality of evil. Yet, mankind was not created to assimilate all the variable aspects of the dark side of evil. Our minds were not designed to hold any negative information or bad memories. *Father God* is a good *Father. He* never intended for us to learn about sin, consider malicious evil, or experience the results of evilness, let alone have thoughts of executing evil deeds.

But, since *Father God* knows the end from the beginning, *He* knew mankind would eventually give in to their curiosity with their self-will and ultimately give in to their free will and disobey Him. Curiosity and their selfish free will had destroyed the best in them, the infilling, perfect glory of their **Most Precious Holy Spirit Eternal Mother.** So, since **Holy Spirit** could no longer abide within **Her** created children, there was a vital requirement to restore those vessels to a position of honor.

In **Genesis,** the Hebrew word for <u>breath</u> is the same as the word <u>spirit</u>. Who will give us that first breath of life if not our mother? The book of **Romans** shows us that we were created for glory. Not our own glory; the glory of our **Most Precious Holy Spirit Mother.** We are blessed to enter into **Her** glory and perfection. This is why **Jesus** was confident in instructing us to be perfect as our **Father God** is perfect. **Jesus** exemplified perfection and knew **Holy Spirit** would come to earth and aid us in this perfection because **She** is the epitome of perfection. *(Matthew 5:48 / Romans 8:18-27)*

Looking into **Proverbs,** *"The spirit of man is the <u>candle</u> of the Lord, searching the inward parts of the belly."* Is not **Holy Spirit** a flame, the fire in our belly, our spirit? <u>Candle</u> means…light, lamp with olive oil, and <u>life</u>. A mother gives life; our **Holy Spirit Mother** birthed us as a spirit being and gave us eternal life in **Her.** *(Genesis 2:7 / Proverbs 20:27 / Romans 9:21-24)*

Father God pre-planned for the **Salvation** of **His** children and the ultimate redemption of **His** created Family. Adam and Eve's selfish free will led them straight toward destruction. But free will was necessary, or **Father God** would have developed mindless robots instead of willing people on earth. Much like mankind, with their grossly evil AI intelligence, is attempting to achieve today. And just what might have made man, those elites in this world, imagine constructing AI? The comparison of AI is another can of worms opened up and found in the **Bible.** *(Joshua 7:12)*

The **Eternal Godhead** wants **Their Family** back together for all eternity. **They** also expect **Their Family** to step up and use our dominion authority forfeited in the Garden. **They** want to place **Their** children back in the Garden of Eden here on earth. And later, after the wedding feast, we will rule over kingdoms.

Once **Jesus, God's** only begotten **Son**, had finished **His** commission, our **Most Precious Holy Spirit** then was able to take **Her** place here on earth to aide us, coming down to earth to counsel, encourage and comfort *Her* redeemed children. *She* did not have to wait any longer. *Holy Spirit* is with us now until the end of this age. Our *Most Precious Holy Spirit Mother* dwells with us, *Her* children, once again, much like the situation in the Garden of Eden. You are your *Mother's child,* after all. We are now reborn, regenerated and renewed with our *Eternal Family. (Genesis 3:22-24 / 1 John 1:7 / Hebrews 12:2 / Acts, Chapters 1-2 / Ephesians 5:18)*

Father and *Son* blessed our *Most Precious Holy Spirit Mother* with this gloriously loving plan to bring us back together. Ultimately, the entire *First Family of God* has each taken part in working together as a *Family* to redeem their created family of mankind. They have always intended for us to be included in *Their* excellent, eternal existence. What more could any child ask of their parents, or their big brother? *(Acts 2:32-33)*

CHAPTER FOURTEEN
the father of lies

That devil, the father of lies, was briefly discussed earlier. A few more telling side points will help you understand the truth presented here. Also relevant, this chapter aids in confirming *God's Most Precious Holy Spirit* is our *Eternal Mother*.

First, are you troubled by the fact that devils roam this earth? Do you fret that a devil might attempt a go at your mind? Let's settle any trepidation you have right now. (And we will refer to the father of lies as it because it is merely a created being, not a person, not a he, merely an it.) *God Almighty* cannot lie; *He* never lies; *He* only tells the truth. That devil only lies; never tells the truth. *Christ Jesus* warned us about the father of lies. <u>The truth versus the lie.</u> Deception began in the Garden and has continued to this day. Whatever *God* has, the devil counterfeits. And not only that, it causes reality to transform into the exact opposite, inventing nothing more than an illusion. *(John 8:44)*

Contrary to *God's Holy Word*, twisting *God's* truth into a lie, that prince of darkness implements evil plans intended to destroy mankind. That cruel father of lies has no intelligence or ability to create anything on the earth or in the air. And its primary goal is to cause as many human beings as possible to stray off the path of truth and be led down a rosy-colored path of nothingness but deception. Causing a human being to accept its lies and become its dupe is an evil thrill for the father of lies. *(Romans 16:18 / 1 Peter 5:8-9)*

The only goal in its agenda is to steal what is true and snake that truth into a lie, coiling around a person's mind and thoughts. That devil doesn't possess the foresight to invent, let alone create from nothing a faked, never before seen or heard of woman/wife/mother goddess out of thin air. The devil only has the ability to take what already has been created, the reality and truth, and then attempt to falsify it with a copycat, inferior, illusionary imitation. *(2 Corinthians 11:13-15)*

The father of lies has taken the truth of the *Godhead* and using this as a model, constructed all kinds of deviations of deities, allowing mankind to pick and choose the god that suits their sinful leanings. Openly exhibited in satanic cultures today are new-age oneness groups, with a love-everyone concept, and those green peace advocates, with their climate change deception, complete with a so-called mother-earth. At the far end of the lying spectrum are secret, evil, cultic ritualistic practices of death, torturing, spilling, and drinking blood in a futile effort to appease the devil, by which conciliation will never happen. With the father of lies, there will never be enough deaths or bloodshed in the world to satisfy its lust for death and destruction of *God's* best creation. *(1 John 3:8)*

That devil attempts at every possible turn to thwart created vessels from becoming infilled with our *Most Precious Holy Spirit Mother.* And it does this by causing people to become confused, accepting false deities, thus granting lesser devils a foothold where they could inhabit people's bodies, minds, and souls. *(1 Timothy 4:1)*

The ultimate goal for any devil is splitting the person apart, thus trapping their spirit. Again, this is a form of imprisonment by a devil. Sad to consider the opposite is the truth, in that a spiritual human being is supposed to be the one in control and commissioned to imprison those devils. See how devils cunningly work to twist up the narrative? Those devils attempt to change the truth into a lie and convince human beings to believe the lie that humans are the weaker ones and destined to become powerless victims. Again, refusing even to acknowledge devils exist can cause an even worse result. Believing that lie when done in fear, not in faith, the person's spirit cannot be filled with *Holy Spirit* or reunited with their *Eternal God Family. (Ephesians 6:11)*

Since the beginning of time, the devil has actively worked through human beings who have been inhabited by devils. Those possessed human beings have been given just enough power, influence, and platforms to become exalted by other human beings as super-intelligent and enlightened. And some of this was done to divert mankind toward other false figures that, sadly, many human beings have subsequently chosen to honor and worship as powerful, female-type deities so-called.

Free will and the demand for self-sufficiency merely result in human beings denying all that is true and righteous. Leaning toward rebellion against *God's* truth and the submissive humility required of a created earthen vessel, a person is free to refuse to accept this truth of being one of *God's* specially designed vessels. In a vicious conglomeration, deception breeds rebellion, and rebellion breeds more deception. Thus, the rebellious deceive themselves, assuming their power has originated from within their self-elating thinking processes and human intelligence. This was the hideous condition of prideful arrogance that the devil, previously named lucifer, exhibited, causing the creature to fall from grace and heaven. *(Isaiah 14:12)*

The truth is, you cannot have it both ways. A person can't fault **Father God** for sending them to hell when they chose to reject being included in **God's Eternal Family** of their free will. It is utter stupidity to demand, "We have intelligence and our free will to choose as we see fit." Then for mankind to accuse **God Almighty** of negligence and error by saying, "Why would **God** be so cruel as to give us a free choice to reject **Him**, causing our eternal loss?" *(Psalms 107:11 / 1 Timothy 4:1)*

Further explaining false deities, numerous false goddesses are found in Greek mythology alone. One stands out above the rest, gaia, the supposed mother of all the earth, referred to as mother-earth. The new age teachings continue to honor gaia, re-enforcing the Greek myth that a false mother goddess of the world here on earth should be revered.

Scripture tells of an idol goddess who was worshipped as the goddess of the fertility of all plant life, dagon, proving the father of lies falsified a goddess-deity who was grounded to the earth. Instead of a heavenly deity, it fabricated a goddess of this earth alone, pointing human beings to stay locked down here, not looking upward to learn of the true **Eternal Deity**. Considering earth to be the end-all-and-be-all in life, one will not concern themselves with the **True Deities** in the eternal heavens. An earth-bound goddess avoids any hint of the true promises of an infinite future with our **God Family** in New Jerusalem that will come down from the heavenly realm. *(Judges 16:1-31)*

Ironically, Greek gods and goddesses have been deemed extremely exaggerated figures, immoral in their self-centered actions, and possessing many character flaws with gross, emotional outbursts. This is an oxymoron since they were labeled supernatural, all-powerful goddesses and gods. Those so-called deities did not possess any form of wisdom and only seemed to produce chaos in the skies. Sad to think mature, adult human beings would accept such flawed, imaginary beings to believe in and give honor to.

It is necessary to note here, too, that satan pointed to mythical gods having family connections, husbands/fathers, wives/mothers, sons, and daughters. However, their families were chaotic mess-ups and quite dysfunctional. Why would the father of lies construct false deities using the family structure? Why would the father of lies use family as the model for gods and goddesses with children in the heavens since it hates the governmental institution of the family on this earth? And why would this be since it actively went about to disrupt and nearly destroy the family unit which **God** created in the Garden of Eden? Why use the unity of family? Just what would be the purpose of doing it? The father of lies has just one reason for doing anything, directing man's attention toward a falsehood, so mankind will give honor to nothing but a mere lie and divert worship away from the truthful **Ones** to worship and honor. *(Psalm 135:15-17)*

Remember, the father of lies can only counterfeit what actually exists; it does not have any ability to create anything from nothing on its own; it is only able to steal its ideas from **God Almighty's** perfect order of creation. Experts don't study a counterfeit dollar; they study the real deal, a minted dollar bill. Contrarily, the devil saw the real deal, the **Eternal Family** and formed a counterfeit replica in those false, godlike, celestial families. The devil did not construct a wholly different form of deity to worship; it used what was already confirmed and in place. And the devil just twisted the truth, adding supernatural gods and goddesses from stars, moon, sun, and planets, and, of course, included their mythical children. This has caused millions of souls to worship the creation, not their **Creator**. Sadly, the devil has convinced religious denominations and nations to accept twisted versions of the true **Deity,** our **Eternal God Family,** labeled the trinity, all considered male, in gender, personality and character.

Ultimately, accepting the perversion of an assumed mother-god deity within the structure of the **Godhead** was a revolting idea for most **God**-fearing, religious sects. So much so that they swung all the way the other way, teaching that the **Godhead** consists of three male entities. And this had much to do with suppressing women within the church hierarchy. Certain **Scripture** verses on women in the church were rashly considered and taken out of context to suit men's agendas. The egotistical nature of men as leaders in the churches caused no small deceptions about women's place in the church. In all actuality, those verses had referred to women speaking out of turn, disrupting meetings with many questions. The majority of the women's questions concerned their confusion over the difference between the false stone statues, gods, and goddesses they were worshipping in temples in their cities, in contrast to what they heard from Paul, Peter and other disciples about **God Almighty**, **Christ Jesus** and their **Most Precious Holy Spirit.** *(1 Corinthians 14:34)*

And it is no coincidence that the father of lies caused men to invent and construct mere, immovable stone statues to be placed in temples of pagan worship. How telling is it that we are earthen vessels infilled with **Holy Spirit's** glory, alive and active! Yet, the gods and goddesses that pagans worship are made of empty stone, locked in temples of stone and mortar. So obvious this is, but the lost seem to be drawn to the immovable, non-living, dead stones, or wooden statues. The father of lies isn't for life, only death. *(Deuteronomy 4:28 / Acts 16:16-34)*

The exceptions are two church sects that have taken up worshiping a false mother-god-deity, major religious organizations, Catholics, and Mormons. This deception and diversion of female goddess worship resurged during the catholic crusades. Various popes were clever in plotting to gain heathen, pagan, god, and goddess worshippers into becoming congregants and signing on to belief in **Christ**. Popes incorporated a Greek-like goddess in the doctrine of their manmade religion. They stuck an insulting goddess title and a false perception of deity onto Mary as being the mother of **God.** Never mind that it was an oxymoron of gross proportions; it worked. *(Luke 1:35 / 2 Thessalonians 2:9-10)*

Catholics teach that Mary is the spiritual mother-god-deity to pray to, which that point in itself is utterly against **Scripture.** However, the devil enjoys seeing this deception continue to play out within Catholic church dioceses. Prayers to Mary are worthless, but most Catholics do not want anything to do with a mystical spirit. They do not understand the exalted place that **Holy Spirit** occupies.

Mormons believe that **God** has a wife, but they do not know who she is and do not consider **Holy Spirit** to be **His Wife**. Amongst other gross misconceptions by the

Mormons are the ideas of having the ability to put forth sacrifice and efforts to become self-appointed, high-level, supernatural beings; having celestial, spirit children of their advanced god-like selves; bringing up a case for the deceased from within their families and getting them saved, by proxy, without the dead ever having to accept **Christ Jesus** on their own, which is nothing more than calling up lying devil spirits, along with the promise of becoming coroneted kings over other planets; to name a shortlist of falsified extremes.

Deception started way back in the Garden with the fall of mankind, and the devil has no new tricks. That father of lies attempts to destroy the family **God** has ordained to rule over the earth in all dominion authority. <u>The father of devils realizes that the less we understand about our true and powerful **Eternal Family** connection, we will never be knowledgeable enough to comprehend the magnitude of our rightful dominion authority and position to rule over the earth and over the devils that creep around on this earth.</u> *(Hosea 4:6)*

As it has played out on earth, its primary purpose for inventing faked deities, including the term trinity, was to divert mankind from knowing the truth about the powerful governmental authority that **God** has <u>invested</u> in **His** earthly family, likened in the image of **His Eternal Godhead Family**. <u>Invested</u> means…bequeathed power and authority bestowed upon someone, authorize, inaugurate.

<u>Questions one might have for the fact devils roam on this earth, and Answers:</u>

- א Q: Why had **God Almighty** allowed this union of human women with fallen angelic beings? A: All were created with their free will. **God** sent the flood to save the earth and mankind by destroying those giants.

- א Q: How did fallen Nephilim beings and human women birth giant children? A: **God Almighty** saw to it those human beings got what they wanted, i.e., strong warrior children by those giants. Many countries use children in their wars even today.

- א Q: How is it that their children are on earth as spirit beings now? A: **God Almighty** stays within **His** ordered plan and eternal circle of creation.

א   Q: Why did **God Almighty and Holy Spirit** place a spirit inside those giant beings? A: **God Almighty** stays within **His** orderly plan for creation and gives whosoever wills the opportunity to be saved. **God** doesn't pick and choose; mankind does.

א   Q: Why had **God** made provision for **His** created angels to reproduce? A: **God Almighty** had given mankind all dominion and authority on earth. Free will is given to all. And **God** foreknew **Christ Jesus** would ultimately reclaim this powerful authority for mankind to subdue the enemy.

א   Q: Had those giants also been given the opportunity to believe in the **God** of all creation? A: Of course, because **Father God** is righteous.

א   Q: Was Cain oppressed by a devil when his anger flared, and he killed his brother? A: Only **Father God** knows.

א   Q: Why was the devil allowed in the Garden of Eden? A: **God** tests everyone; read about Job's life.

God's order and plan for **His** created beings runs consistently through life and birth, including our eternal spirits. Even angels have free will and are immortal, too, so it holds true all the way down the line of creation. And though **God** knew they would be born as giants in the land, **He** gave them the same opportunity as all human beings who choose to accept or reject **God.** No one, especially not angels, will be able to accuse **God Almighty** of not giving them ample opportunities to experience eternal life with **His Family.**

Christ Jesus had to deal with devils, and **He** sent them fleeing every single time. However, **Jesus** did not eradicate those devils who continue to harass human beings. **Jesus** was an obedient **Son** and only did or said what **His Father** instructed **Him** to do or say. So, we know that it was not within the realm of **Father God's** purpose or **Christ Jesus'** commission to include the imprisonment of devils on this earth during **His** mission. And notice that in **Revelation, Chapter 19, King Yehowshua** will eliminate those evil kings and mighty men who have set themselves against **His Father God's Family.** However, nothing is mentioned about those devils roaming this earth. Why is this? Then in **Revelation, Chapter 20, King Yehowshua** will imprison the father of lies for one thousand years. (*Genesis 1:26-28)*

Though there is no contest between the devil and **God Almighty**, the devil remains full of revenge against **God.** And that devil plans to destroy as much of **God's** creation as possible. Paradoxically, because the father of lies knows its time is short, that devil is doing its worst to capture as many earthen vessels as possible, stealing them from their **Father God** and destroying them.

Remember, that father of devils actively attempts to twist the narrative and imprison human beings' spirits. The devil endeavors to lock us down in chains of bondage before we comprehend that we hold all the power that heaven affords us to place those devils that are roaming around on this earth in chains. And so, its imps aggressively plot to sneak into any receptive earthen vessel, and confuse them, before a human being grasps their powerful dominion authority. The devil is desperate for us not to realize our commission on this earth as the ruling children of the **Most High God**.

The fact is the gates to the Garden of Eden were closed by the cherubim and then kept guarded to preserve the Garden for the wedding feast to come. And so, with that closure, the father of lies thought it had won a major victory; mankind was driven out, no longer under **God's** protective wing. Mankind was then forced to live on the devil's turf. The father of lies had gained easy access to earthen vessels for twisting the truth and confusing mankind. That lead devil, that evil father of lies, likes prideful idiots because its imps can turn those earthen vessels into dummies, their personal puppets.

But! **God Almighty** had already looked ahead and saw the end from the beginning. **He** had a plan! That sneaky devil wasn't so clever after all and definitely not even close to its **Creator, God Almighty**. Those imps are confused by their own lies and always end up falling into their own traps. Whatever the father of lies thinks it accomplished returns on its own head. **Salvation, Christ Jesus'** death and resurrection were just that way. *(Genesis 3:15)*

And so, what needs to be done with those evil spirits now roaming this earth, not having any place to settle? **Jesus** understood that on this earth, we hold this position of authority. **He** showed this truth to **His** disciples when **He** sent out the seventy-two evangelists, and they marveled that devils were subject to them. *Jesus* answered that it was no big deal that devils were subject to their words and commands. Within this threefold purpose for mankind, all dominion authority has been given to us to meet with *God Almighty* and strategize with *Him*. Then we are to order angels to arrest and imprison those enemies of our *Lord* to be the footstool for *Christ Jesus* when *He* returns. *Christ Jesus* asked, *"Nevertheless when the Son of man cometh, shall He find faith on the earth?"* Faith trusts *Father God Almighty* to be completely honest with us, eagerly listening to that *'still small voice,'* and then heeding instructions from *God Almighty. (Psalm 110:1 / Luke 18:8 / Luke 10:17-21 / Hebrews 1:14)*

The word <u>bind</u> in the New Testament points us to the truth about our *God-given* dominion authority to subdue devils. *Christ Jesus* promised *His* disciples that they would do greater things than *He* had done on earth, which is one aspect of those greater things. Why is this? *Christ Jesus* was not commissioned to eradicate devils off the earth; mankind has been granted this task, to subdue all that creeps on this earth. *He* said, *"Whatsoever ye <u>bind</u> on earth shall be bound in heaven: and whatsoever ye shall <u>loose</u> on earth shall be loosed in heaven."* <u>Bind</u> means…to tie up, to imprison in bonds. This is part of our commission to command angel hosts/armies to arrest devils and imprison them. <u>Loose</u> means…to untie, release, and break off. This, too, is part of our commission, destiny, and purpose, to deliver human vessels blinded by lies, breaking off the chains that devils have put on them, setting those vessels free to again live in unity with their families and peacefully with the *Eternal Family of God. (Genesis 1:26 / Matthew 18:18)*

There is another type of <u>binding</u> found in the Old Testament. *Jesus* read a verse from *Isaiah 61:1*; during *His* formal address to Jewish leaders when *He* stood in the Jewish synagogue, *"The Spirit of the Lord God is upon Me because the Lord hath anointed Me to preach good tidings unto the meek; He hath sent Me to <u>bind</u> up the brokenhearted, to proclaim <u>liberty</u> to the <u>captives</u>, and the opening of the prison to them that are bound…"* <u>Bind</u> means…to wrap, to bandage. <u>Liberty</u> means…freedom from slavery, family land restored. <u>Captives</u> means…captive prisoners. *(Isaiah 61:1)*

Just know that we also have the power to heal, set at liberty captives bound by sin through *Christ Jesus*, and even have land and property returned to families under *God's* covenant.

And as created earthen vessels, we were built in physical form to house an invisible, immortal spirit-being. **God's** plan for us is to accommodate the best **Spirit Being, Holy Spirit.** However, going into eternity, be assured that each of us will be harboring some type of powerful, invisible to the naked eye, spirit-being. Nothing created is neutral or self-actuating, meaning that we are not creatures living creatively or fully all on our own apart from **God Almighty, El Shaddi.**

This is **God Almighty's** order for **His** creation of mankind. And so it shall be that we ultimately will be occupied. We ultimately will be occupied; spirit must line up with spirit because flesh and blood cannot contain spirit infilling or attain eternal life with **God.** If one's spirit isn't aligned with **Holy Spirit**, then that physical body will be used against itself by housing a counterfeit false spirit, imprisoning that person's spirit. *(John 3:6)*

The father of lies is only able to twist the truth of **God's** order into a falsified version of reality. The truth is we are empty vessels to be filled up. Once a vessel becomes inhabited by one of its devils, that vessel is then forced to do their dirty work. Man's rejection of **God's Family** and **Their** eternal love offered calls for justice for that vessel. In their free will, mankind has the option to choose to remain apart from **God.** So, **God Almighty** grants a rebellious vessel what he/she wants, complete voided space far from the **Eternal Godhead.**

Man's rejection of the presence of **God** is realized to the fullest at the time of man's death. That one is lost for all eternity. **God** would have included that one if only that created vessel had freely chosen to admit to having been made and then would have honored the **Godhead Who** created them and accepted their rightful place in **Father God's Eternal Family.** Hell is the only place **God Almighty** created that is available for such a one to go off to, whosoever has renounced their birthright to return to the presence of **God.** Hell was originally reserved for the father of lies. The equation below shows the fall of such a vessel because of sinfulness, thus destroying that man or woman.

The sad reality of mankind who reject the purpose for which they were created:

snake/serpent~358 + man~45 + sin~418 + rejection~101 + truth~441 + lack~42 + knowledge~474 + lost~7 + birthright~227 = **2,113** satan~359 + <u>witness</u>~2 + <u>mankind</u>~45 + <u>death</u>~446 + <u>soul</u>~430 + <u>perish</u>~49 + <u>hell</u>~337 + <u>fire</u>~301 + <u>eternity</u>~144 = **2,113**

Like with Job's testing experience, the father of lies looks for an opportunity with any soul to get them to curse **God.** That one is lost forever, and thus, **God Almighty** must honor one's free will and send the lost soul away because satan witnessed them rejecting the presence of **God** their **Father. (Job 1:8-12)**

That devil operates stealthily by lying and confusing a person who independently chooses their own path in an attempt to achieve an autonomous eternal existence. And those who assume there is no eternal realm, like professed atheists, will be doubly surprised upon their deaths. The father of lies convinces some rebellious ones to believe in numerous paths to attain eternal reality instead of listening to the absolute truth. Not accepting the loving sacrifice of the firstborn, our elder brother, **Christ Jesus,** took on, in that all of **His** pain and suffering was done just for us, is shameful. It is the rejection of true love at its worst. **He** lovingly and willingly accepted our crimes, shame, and punishment. Not accepting His forgiveness and regeneration into the **Eternal Family of God** would be damning. **(Psalm 73:6-18 / Matthew 7: 13-14 / John 14:6 / Colossians 1:13-15)**

<u>The sad reality of one in pride, thinking they are more intelligent than</u> *God,* **<u>is</u>** **<u>assuming they have answers to eternal life apart from the life</u>** *God Almighty* **<u>offers:</u>**

<u>devil</u>~304 + <u>snake/serpent</u>~358 + <u>chaos/confusion</u>~702 + <u>truth</u>~441 + ***<u>YAHWEH</u>***~26 + <u>steal</u>~55 + <u>son</u>~52 + <u>lost</u>~7 = **1,945**

<u>mankind</u>~45 + <u>lie</u>~29 + <u>soul</u>~430 + <u>truth</u>~441 + <u>life</u>~18 + <u>perish</u>~49 + <u>groan</u>~151 + <u>hell</u>~337 + <u>fire</u>~301 + <u>eternity</u>~144 = **1,945**

Sadly, these equations clearly explain the warning through **God's** perfect language that rebellion, pride, and rejection dooms a person to the place reserved for the father of lies.

<u>Its tactics are nothing more than tricks by the devil to imprison mankind and take them down to hell with it.</u>

CHAPTER FIFTEEN
MAKING AN END OF EVIL ACROSS THE EARTH

We were made in **Their Image**. We can experience all **They** have, as long as we are obedient, functioning within **Their** perimeters for us as **Their** chosen vessels filled up with the **Most Precious Holy Spirit** to work and flow out through us. Vessels can only pour out what is poured into them. We must be clean, new wineskins to contain the pure, intoxicating ether, that pure wine of **Holy Spirit,** which will bring joy, peace, and love to all human beings in complete harmony with the eternal realm upon this earth. This will be better than any wine made by man. **Jesus** even referred to mankind as becoming new wineskins. *(Matthew 9:17 / Mark 2: 22 / John 8:44 / Acts 17:29 / 2 Timothy 2:21)*

By being willing vessels containing the **Most Precious Holy Spirit,** allowing **Her** to have **Her** way to will and work goodness in this world in and through us, we truly become **Her** hands and feet on earth. The best way to aid in ending poverty, child abuse, abortion, wars, thefts, killings, greed, sexual lusts, and perversions, etc., is to be obedient unto the point of the death of our self-will. Emptying ourselves of all else is our dutiful position now, and becoming just like **Christ Jesus**, an obedient child of **God**, only doing and saying what we have been instructed to do and say. **Father and Mother** know best where, when, how to place us and who to place us with to accomplish these supernatural goals. *(Acts 1:8 / John 16:7-15)*

This world will only be righted when only goodness prevails. Only one is all good and worthy of praise. And **Jesus** said unto them, *"Why callest thou, Me good? There is none good but One, that is God." Christ Jesus* had made this remark openly because **He** was called the son of man, so **He** could complete **His** purpose as our substitute to die in our place. Too, **He** was not going to give away **His** purpose to the father of lies. *(Mark 10:18)*

The truthful **One**, worthy of all glory and praise, to be worshipped, revered, honored, and given homage to is our **Father God Almighty** of the **Eternal Family**. Even **Jesus** and **Holy Spirit** honor **God Almighty**. *(1 Timothy 1:17 / Revelation 4:11)*

In reference to the term, mother-of-god, who is this person, Mary, the woman who had carried **Christ Jesus** in her womb? Regarding Mary not being included in the deity of the

Godhead, she indeed was *God's* chosen vessel to be the surrogate mother of *Jesus* when *He* was destined to come to earth in the flesh. *God* searched the earth to find a humble person and found Mary. However, Mary was no different from each person ever created to be a vessel. Mary was, as we are, a created vessel of honor to house *God's Most Precious Holy Spirit.*

Briefly discussed was the truth that *Father God and His Wife, Jesus' Mother Holy Spirit,* visited Mary's womb. In all purity and holiness, *They* were together, and this union caused Mary's womb to be infilled with the body of the *Spirit Being, Yehowshua,* as the surrogate mother for *Their Son,* to produce a body of flesh that perfect *Lamb* equivalent and sacrifice. All of life is a miracle created by *God Almighty!* We cannot fully understand this and cannot create a baby independently; we only take part in this miracle of physical life being formed in the womb. That baby, not yet breathing on its own, and growing into a multifunctioning body independent of its mother inside the womb, is too complex to understand fully. Yet, *They* make it happen and give that creation a jumpstart spark with the light of life. *Christ Jesus* stated that *He* is the *Light* and the *Life.* The entire *Eternal Family of God* were all three present and involved with the *Salvation* plan. *(Luke 1:35 / John 8:12 / John 14:6)*

Father God made man from dust; creation is entirely within *God's* ability. *God Almighty* causes the conception of our physical bodies and has known each of us before we entered the womb of our human mother. A powerful lightning spark of life and our spirits are infused in us. This gift of life is a miracle and is beyond our natural mind's comprehension. In perfect form, like a strong threefold cord, our body is the image of *Christ Jesus,* our elder brother, our spirit is in the likeness of *Holy Spirit,* and our soul is the creation of the morally good, right-thinking part of the conscience of *Father God Almighty.* And this brings up the point of why it is vital to protect our minds, not pervert our thoughts with the knowledge of evil. Again, *Father God* has only ever wanted good for us, all goodness, only joy, peace, and happiness. *(Psalm 139:14)*

God's chosen vessel, Mary, was human, conceived from mortal man and required *Salvation* as any other person. She is not the deity who came to earth, not a goddess; she too needed to be able to return to live for eternity with *God.* She had the exact fallen nature that all mankind possesses since the sin and fall of Adam and Eve.

In **Genesis 1:2,** this verse points to our **Most Precious Holy Spirit Mother**'s involvement in creating the earth and thus all mankind. **She** was hovering over and breathing upon the earth, giving us the breath of life. This is exactly like our human mothers do with our physical bodies when we are in our mother's womb; they provide our oxygen. In this perfect analogy, as a mother hen will hover over her eggs in anticipation of the birth of her chicks, **Holy Spirit** hovered over the face of the earth. **Qodesh Ruach**, reviewing the Hebrew name for **Holy Spirit** means...holy, pure, set apart, sanctified... and ...the immaterial spirit part, wind, breath, and the seat of life. This references a supernatural **Spirit Mother**, our **Most Precious Holy Spirit Mother. (Qodosh Ruach/Strong's Concordance #6918 / #7307)**

Once more, in the subsequent verse in **Genesis, God Almighty** said, **"Let US make mankind in OUR IMAGE."** That is a statement by **God Almighty,** speaking of plural deities, not only of the **Father** and the **Son** but also of our **Father and Mother. Father God** did not first create a man as a father and then create another man as his son. Nope. **God** created man first as a husband and then created woman as his wife. **God's** moral law for all human life is first, the marital state, then beginning a family by conception and birth. This is how morally the <u>multiplication</u> of **God's** created vessels occurs. <u>Multiply</u> means...to grow in number, to bear offspring. **(Genesis 1:26)**

And **Jesus** said unto them, *"For the hardness of your hearts he (Moses) wrote you this precept. But, from the beginning of creation, **God** made them both male and female. For this cause shall a man leave his father and mother and cleave to his wife. And they twain shall be one flesh; so they are no more twain, but one flesh. What therefore **God** hath joined together, let not man put asunder."* This has forever been **God's** mandate for the marriage covenant and the most secure way for children to be reared when they come into this world. **(Mark 10:5-9)**

According to **God's** pure laws of morality, **Father God** could never have been a fornicator or adulterer with the human woman, Mary. **Father God** works within **His** order and law of the marriage covenant. It is unthinkable that **God** would have cohabited with Mary, a young virgin, betrothed to another man. And too, Mary's natural functions, i.e., an egg from her fallen human nature, could not have been used to form *Jesus* in the flesh, <u>*the*</u> <u>**One** *Who became the pure, spotless, sacrificial* **Lamb** *in the flesh.* *(John 1:29)*</u>

Just as we can accept our **Lord God Almighty** is our heavenly **Father, Christ Jesus' Father,** and **Jesus is His Son** and our elder brother, the firstborn of many brethren; we must then follow **God's** law of morality and **His** institution of marriage and family that **God Himself** created in **Their Image and Likeness. (Romans 8:29)**

Does it make sense that **Father God** would solely be the **Father** of **Jesus** as a single father? Is **God** a step-father with **Jesus** being **His** only begotten **Son**? Did **Father God Almighty** give birth to **His Son** as a transgender father? Nope! Those types of father figures are not possibilities to even be considered. And we can fully accept the truth that **God** would never go outside of **His** order of birthing a child in either of these ways. We must acknowledge then that **God Almighty** is **Father** to **His** only <u>begotten</u> **Son, Jesus**. According to **God's** moral laws and marriage covenant law, **He** had to have begotten **His Son** by initially being a faithful, loving **Husband** within the mandate of **His** moral law of the marriage covenant before becoming a **Father**. <u>Begotten</u> means…one and only, unique. *(John 3:16 / John 1:18)*

To settle any issue concerning questions or arguments of pronoun usage, **Scripture** does read in several places of **Holy Spirit** as being 'he' 'his' 'he will show you' as seen in the following **Scripture** verse. *"But the **Comforter**, which is **Holy Spirit, whom** the **Father** will send in **My** name, **He** shall teach you all things and bring all things to your remembrance, whatsoever **I** have said unto you."*

A father teaches his children, but a mother teaches her children as well to remember what their father has instructed them by urging them towards good works. **Father God** instructed **Jesus** to share the truth that **He** would send **His Spirit** to earth to pass instructions on to us after coming into that upper room at Pentecost and now residing with us and in us. *(John 14:26 / Acts 2:1-4)*

Looking closely at these pronouns, he, she, it, the archaic pronoun usage was lost long ago in translation. Only one word was used for the three individual pronouns in the original Hebrew. These Hebrew letters are hey-wow-shuruq-aleph and pronounced <u>hoo</u>. Many years later, after **Christ Jesus** walked this earth, scribes of Hebrew texts revised **hoo,** initially used for all three pronoun genders, to finally distinguish between male and female genders for readers of Hebrew. The pronoun hoo remained the pronoun word for the male gender pronouns for he, him, and his. And the new pronoun hee became the pronoun word for the feminine gender pronouns she, her, and hers. The letters used in modern versions are hey-yod-hiriq-aleph, pronounced hee for the pronoun she. Again, hoo is used for he, him, his; hee is used for she, her, hers.

It is appropriate to consider the pronoun which **Christ Jesus** used when **He** spoke concerning the **Comforter** would have been in the original Hebrew vernacular, that is, the one word used for all three pronouns, she, he, or it, which was hoo. **Christ Jesus** would likely have spoken perfect, archaic Hebrew whenever **He** spoke, to the great surprise of scholarly Pharisees, who also were very familiar with the original Paleo form. They were astonished that **Christ Jesus** could read a scroll. So, speaking of **His Mother,** and possibly, to not give away the truth of **Her** reality to those vipers and whitewashed tombs, who would have refused the truth anyway, hoo was quite possibly used by **Jesus** for this archaic pronoun when referring to **His Eternal Mother. (Matthew 23:27-28 / Luke 4: 16-22)**

CHAPTER SIXTEEN
FATHER GOD AND MOTHER GOD

Now let's explore the facts of this precise connection between the aleph and beth. We have established that Hebrew is the language of **God Almighty**. Mankind spoke Hebrew/Ibree until the tower of Babel. As you've witnessed, this beautiful language laid out in this text is full of complementary truths with deeper meanings. In the Strong's Concordance, the first letter noted in the Hebrew alphabet is aleph, and that letter also stands for **He** and **Him**. Yet! Also presented is another meaning for aleph, that being **She**, and **Her**.

Father God has given the honor to **His Wife** and has put **Her** first within the Hebrew aleph-beth. On the first page of Strong's Hebrew Concordance, top left column of the page, #0.1, it's the first Hebrew letter given. Please note that the pronouns he and him/she and her do not begin with capital letters in the Strong's Concordance. Capital letters are never used in Hebrew, not even when writing proper names. Capital letters in this text are done for emphasis to give our **God Family** the honor that is due **Them**.

Triple proofs that *God Almighty* is married to *His Bride/Wife/Holy Spirit*:

oneness/aleph~*1* + **God**~45 + pleasure~346 + love~285 + **Wife/Spouse**~55 + union/beth~2 + seven spirits of **God**~7 + glory~32 = **773**

oneness/aleph~*1* + **God/YAHWEH**~26 + **Bride/Spouse**~55 + **Holy Spirit**~624 + seven spirits of **God**~*7* + married~20 + love~8 + glory~32 = **773**

oneness/aleph~*1* + **Bride/**qof~100 + wisdom(woman in **Proverbs**)~73 + perfection~490 + seven spirits of **God**~7 + married~20 + love~13 + glory~32 + magnified~37 = **773**

Resolution 773:

(7) completed perfection, **Holy Spirit** carries the seven spirits of **God**

(7) rest, the seed of the **Father**, and new life by the **Mother**

(3) divinity, *One God*, three parts of a person, spirit, soul, body, and gifts given

This equation and resolution provide evidence that **Holy Spirit Mother** is wed to **Almighty Father God**. Their marriage is the perfection of a union, full of love and wisdom; it is our shining example of the marriage covenant, the most excellent love two persons can have for one another. *God Almighty* ordained that man and woman are no more twain, but one, and too, what *God* has joined together, let no man separate. Remember, *Holy Spirit* has been sent to earth! *(Revelation 5:6)*

Not to belabor these pronouns, though it is necessary to note that the first two letters of the Hebrew aleph-beth, the aleph and the beth, refer to both masculine and feminine genders. (#1, first page, the third letter from the top, in the Strong's Hebrew Dictionary)

This name, **_Comforter_**, was spoken of by **Christ Jesus** in the book of **John**. What comes to mind when reading about the **Comforter**? Obviously, a mother, of course. Mothers <u>comfort</u> their children. Mothers <u>encourage</u> their children and <u>counsel</u> their children. And too, mothers will <u>intercede</u> on behalf of their children with their fathers. Motherly attributes comprise the direct meanings and definitions of the word **Comforter** in *Scripture*. **_Comforter_** means…intercessor, helper, encourager, comforter, counselor, and advocate. *(John 15:26)*

Another verse that **Jesus** spoke was a severe warning about disrespecting the **Holy Spirit**. *"Wherefore I say unto you, All manner of sin and blasphemy shall be forgiven unto men: but the blasphemy against the Holy Ghost shall not be forgiven unto men."* **Jesus** warned that neither **He** nor **Father God** would tolerate speaking against **Their Most Precious Holy Spirit Wife and Mother**, respectively. **He** stated this fact emphatically, just like any loving son would defend his mother if someone spoke ill of her. *(Matthew 12:31)*

Our **Most Precious Holy Spirit Mother** gives wonderfully unique gifts to her children. Mothers love to bless their children, surprising them. Once being cleansed vessels, new wineskins, infilled with our **Mother Holy Spirit's** ethereal flow, we can obediently operate in those gifts. With our **Mother's** urging, we are doubly blessed to have received these perfect gifts to share **Her** supernatural power to bless others with those gifts. *(1 Corinthians 12:4-10)*

Holy Spirit gives gifts to Her children for the healing of the nations:

1) The Gift of the Word of Wisdom

2) The Gift of the Word of Knowledge

3) The Gift of Faith

4) The Gift of Healing

5) The Gift of Working Miracles

6) The Gift of Prophecy

7) The Gift of Discerning between spirits, good or evil

8) The Gift of Tongues, Different Languages

9) The Gift of Interpretation of Tongues/Languages

Our *Holy Spirit Mother* teaches good manners to her children as all good mothers would. The fruit of *Holy Spirit* within a person's mature character exemplifies an obedient, respectful child exhibiting good manners and kindness. What a complete list of virtuous fruit in a child filled with their *Mother Holy Spirit*! Like *Mother,* like child! *(Galatians 5:22-23)*

Our *Eternal Mother* teaches us good manners that produce virtues:

1) Love

2) Joy

3) Peace

4) Patience/Longsuffering

5) Gentleness/Kindness

6) Goodness/Servanthood

7) Faithfulness/Loyalty

8) Meekness/Humility

9) Temperance/Self-control

Revelation, Chapter 12, speaks directly of a certain woman, not a mere parallel or symbolic woman figure. If you still have doubts about this truth, read it over again; the woman in this chapter is the ***Holy Spirit***. This is also the same ***Woman*** written about in ***Genesis 3:15; Her Son's*** heel being bruised, and the serpent's head being crushed, this ***Eternal Being, Holy Spirit,*** is ***One*** of the ***Godhead***. This ***Woman*** spoken of in that chapter is ***Eternal Mother Holy Spirit, Mother*** of all people on the earth, and ***Christ Jesus, Her Son.*** These verses refer to ***Him*** specifically as the child of ***Holy Spirit***, not of Joseph's wife, Mary, and not of Eve, Adam's wife, the mother of all human beings,

Chapters 1 and 2 of *Acts*, Chapter 12 of *Revelation* share the truth of the ***Family of God*** and that ***God's Wife, Holy Spirit,*** has been sent to earth and will remain here until ***Christ Jesus*** returns. And ***She*** will be hidden away, protected, housed, and nourished during the tribulation here on earth; *"And the **Woman** fled into the wilderness, where **She** hath a place prepared of **God**, that they (angels) should feed **Her** there one-thousand-two-hundred-and-threescore days."* ***(Revelation 12:6)***

So, rest easy, child of the ***Eternal God Almighty***. We are assured that we will be protected and kept safe because ***She*** is here now on earth and indwelling us! Remember; we were in our ***Eternal Mother***, and now ***She*** is not only close to us to care for us but is in reality in-filling us with joy and peace! How much more caring can our ***Holy Spirit Mother*** show that ***She*** loves us than this? When ***She*** is transported and hidden away, all saints of ***God*** will be hidden away, the bridal party, those five virgins with oil, and guests going into the wedding feast. That oil spoken of is the anointing oil keeping our lights lit and is of our ***Holy Spirit Mother***. So, do you have this oil? Isn't it a sweet coincidence that mothers rub their babies down with oils after a cleansing bath? Nope. No coincidence here at all. Everything on earth points to the truth of the eternal all around us. Do you watch for these examples?

CHAPTER SEVENTEEN
WHISKED AWAY TO SAFETY

Let's continue with these protective qualities that **Holy Spirit** has resident in **Her** personality. Who feeds her children? A good mother provides her children with healthy, sustaining food with great nutrition that gives them sustenance. *"He that hath an ear, let him hear what the **Spirit** saith unto the churches; To him that overcometh will I give to eat of the tree of life, which is in the midst of the <u>paradise</u> of **God**."* Our **Savior** and **King**, speaking to John in the book of **Revelation,** referred to **His Holy Spirit Mother** about once again providing mankind food from that guarded tree of life! **Christ Jesus** also spoke of <u>paradise</u> to the thief on the cross next to Him. Our beloved family members, who have died, are waiting for the millennial reign in the Garden of Eden. They have not gone up to heaven. They are still here on earth in spirit form and will one day be called forth by our **King** of kings when **He** returns, the same as **Christ Jesus** called Lazarus forth. <u>Paradise </u> means…in the Greek concordance section…a place of blessedness, paradise, a garden. *(Luke 23:43 / John 11:38-44 / Revelation 2:7)*

We will be in the Garden of Eden once again! The life-giving food for the eternal life of **God's** children will be made available once more. **Most Precious Holy Spirit Eternal Mother** will give food to **Her** children in the Garden of Eden. Though the Garden is on this earth, now the devil's turf, cherubim have securely protected that special place for millennia. So that is one area where the father of lies can no longer sneak into. And shortly, listening and obedient saints of **God Almighty** will have angels arresting all devil spirits as they begin taking back dominion control of this land.

And, if you are wondering about that occurrence with the devil sneaking in like a serpent, consider Job. **God Almighty** allowed the devil to perform the testing of Job. Job knew of **God,** but after being tested, he knew **God**. That's a big difference! We must all endure tests; even school teaches us this. Research scientists must corroborate their theories with numerous blind research tests. Job was tested, and you, too, could probably point out some testing you have experienced in your life.

Not much, if any, of the following has been taught:

א The **Lord God Almighty** created the Garden of Eden to be the lush paradise where **Holy Spirit** will place **Her** vessels of honor, eternal mankind spirit beings.

א **Holy Spirit** will not leave us on earth alone during the tribulation but will protect **God's** children who have **His** name and mark; they will be hidden away on this earth.

א We will not leave this earth during the tribulation (3 ½ years) but will be kept safe here on earth in the Garden of Eden.

א During the time (3 ½ years) of wrath, we will be attending the wedding feast within the Garden of Eden, an outdoor venue, **Christ Jesus'** wedding feast. **(Psalm 23 / Revelation 12)**

א **God's** cherubim have guarded the Garden of Eden for 2,000+ years, and they are still in front of those gates, guarding, waiting for the wedding feast and for mankind to gain reentrance by going from glory to glory, having on our white robes of righteousness, once again covering our nakedness.

א Those disciples who have not tasted death until **Christ Jesus** returns, as He hinted, might be waiting it out there in the Garden of Eden, protected and fed by the angels like Elijah was fed when in a cave. **(1 Kings 17:6 / Matthew 16: 27-28)**

Equation proving the children of *Father God* will be hidden away, as written in *Revelation, Chapters 3 and 12*:

Yahweh/God~26 + hand~14 + angels~91 + garden~53 + feed~275 + **Mother**~41 + eternal~144 + spirit~214 + hidden~388 + wilderness~246 = **1,492**

eden~124 + eternal~144 + spirit~214 + clothed~332 + white~82 + kept~540 + nourished~56 = **1,492**

Resolution 1,492:

(1) unity with the *Godhead*

(4) open gate to the entrance of Eden

(9) finished work

(2) witness and testimony of *Yehowshua's Salvation*

Our omnipresent *God Almighty, Who* is everywhere at all times and will oversee *His* angels, for *His Wife* and children as they are hidden away; the ones with their witness of accepting the free gift of *Salvation* by *Yehowshua*, with their oil lamps full of the fire of *Holy Spirit*, with mature fruit and gifts operating, and with *Father God's* name written on them.

Amazing proof of the hidden place of safety during the tribulation:

Hey! Behold! Look! <u>he</u>~5 + **<u>Bride</u>**~55 + <u>mark</u>~406 + **God/<u>YAHWEH</u>**~26 + <u>fled</u>~210 + <u>wilderness</u>~246 + <u>eden</u>~124 + <u>hidden</u>~388 + <u>kingdom</u>~135= **1,595**

<u>espousal</u>~463 + <u>faith</u>~102 + <u>kept</u>~540 + <u>hour</u>~375 + <u>temptation</u>~105 + kingdom/<u>yod</u>~10 = **1,595**

Resolution 1,595:

(1) unity with our *Eternal Father*

(5) breath of eternal life given to us by *Holy Spirit Mother*

(9) testing comes to an end for the child, by finished work of *Christ Jesus*

(5) grace extended to mankind by *Father God Almighty*

The *Bride, Father God's Wife, Holy Spirit*, poor in spirit, meaning full of perfect humility, with the name and mark of *God Almighty* on *Her*, will flee into the wilderness of Eden and will be hidden and kept from the hour of temptation for 3 ½ years. And, as we've seen in *Scripture*, as well as in these equations, *Holy Spirit* will take *God's* children with *Her*. *Father God* is also involved, and restoration was made possible by the blood sacrifice of *Yehowshua!* And yes, *Holy Spirit* is shown to be there in the book of *Revelation* at the very beginning in Chapter 1 and at the end of Chapter 22 because *She* is here on earth and will remain here until *King Yehowshua* returns to reign. *Holy Spirit* will not leave earth during the tribulation but will cover *Her* children like a hen covers her chicks under her wing to protect them as *She* had done at the beginning of the creation of the earth. With angels assisting, *She* will transport us to safety and hide us away with *Her,* like it is written in *Revelation, Chapters 3 and 12.*

Again, it is good to mention that as *Christ Jesus* hung on that rugged cross, *He* made a promise to the thief hanging next to *Him*, the man who believed *Jesus* is the *Savior* of the world, by asking *Jesus* to remember him when *He* came into *His* kingdom. *And Jesus said unto him, Verily I say unto thee, Today shalt thou be with Me in paradise." (Luke 23:43)*

Consider once more, the word <u>paradise.</u> This is the Garden of Eden that *Father God* has preserved and reserved since the beginning of time and for all of these millennia. <u>Paradise</u> means…a place of blessedness, a garden. Why else would *God* have cherubim come from heaven to earth to guard the entrance of the Garden of Eden? *(Matthew 6:13 / John 17:15 / Revelation 3:10 and Chapter 12)*

What a wonderful truth revealed to know that when our *Eternal Mother Holy Spirit* will be whisked away to safety where the angels, who will be sent to earth to minister to the sons of *God*, will care for Her and us, we will be whisked along with *Her* to the Garden because *She* resides within us now. That's the only way for each of us to attain a peaceful eternal life. We could never achieve an eternal, healthy, unhindered, blissful, forevermore existence on our own. We aren't self-created gods unto ourselves. And we sure wouldn't be able to sneak into the Garden and grab fruit off the tree of eternal life for wholeness and happiness. And again, we do get to choose where we will go for eternity. *(Hebrews 1:13-14 /Revelation 22:2)*

And! It is glorious to learn that we were created as a spirit able to contain the immortal life of *Holy Spirit.* Well, how about this! We are wired this way, after all! In the likeness of the threefold *Godhead*, we are valid recipients of *God's* loving and creative plan for *His Wife* and meant to be beautifully formed, earthen clay vessels for *Her* to inhabit and move and have *Her Being* in and through. As long as we stick by our *Mother,* we will be fine.

She knows how to keep **Her** houses in order, vessels of honor who carry our **Most Precious Holy Spirit Eternal Mother** within us. We are fulfilled by being our **Mother's** hands, feet, and heart, exhibiting **Her** love on this earth.

We, these chosen vessels, created by the **Lord God Almighty** for **His** good pleasure, reborn in the **Spirit**, cleansed, new wineskin vessels, carry the **Most Precious Holy Spirit's** intoxicating wine to pour out onto all people who accept their place in the **Eternal Family of God**, made possible through the blood-bought provision of **Their Son, Christ Jesus.** Our elder **Brother, Christ Jesus,** did it all for us and redeemed us back to **His Eternal God Family.** Like our **Mother**, we are to pour out that excellent, living, and active new wine which **She** offers to all, characterized as Joy, Peace, Patience, Gentleness, Goodness, Faith, Humility, Self-control, and Love.

There are many other proofs in **Scripture** that point to the **Lord God Almighty, His** House, **His** Land/Earth, **His** plan for **Family, His** plan for the **Salvation** of all mankind, and **His Creation in Their** likeness and image. And here are more mathematical proofs as well.

Revisiting, YAHWEH + HOLY SPIRIT + YEHOWSHUA = GODHEAD:

Godhead~1,399 + unity~22 + **Word**~206 + create~203 + speak~206 + life~18 = **2,054**

love~8 + joy~353 + unity~22 + speak~206 + **Word**~206 + music~510 + enter~9 + wind~214 + fire~301 + light~207 + life~18 = **2,054**

A third proof confirming proof that mankind is to be infilled with our _Holy Spirit, Eternal Mother,_ the physical portrait of the _Godhead:_

mankind/vav~6 + life~18 + seven-spirits-infilling~586 + **_Eternal Mother_**~444 + wisdom~73 + truth~441 + knowledge~474 + government~12 = **2,054**

Resolution 2,054:

(2) our witness of the **God Family** for all eternity

(0) the *Eternal Family* circle unbroken in eternity

(5) grace extended to mankind

(4) gate, door reopened to mankind

Mankind's eternal life is included in the equation of the *Eternal Godhead.* We were always planned for, meant to fit seamlessly into *God's* scheme of things with *His* creation plan, family plan and loving plan for the continuance of *His* ever-expanding creation.

God's universal purpose for mankind:

head~501 + *Eternal*~144 + *Family*~433 + *Father/God/Yahweh*~45 + good~17 + pleasure~346 + married~20 + unity~22 + union/beth~2 + glory~32 + *Holy Spirit*~624 + *Mother*~41 + water~90 + light~207 + fire~301 + wind~214 + *Yehowshua*~391 + crowned~620 + dominion~209 + authority~580 + mouth~85 + speak~206 + *Word*~206 + love~8 + formed~300 + mankind~45 + image~160 + family~433 = **6,282**

Mankind's detailed purpose within *God's* universal purpose:

sanctified~404 + image~160 + unity~22 + salt~78 + light~207 + fire~301 + glory~32 + sing~341 + shout~300 + sound~136 + joy~353 + worship~313 + *YAHWEH*~26 + kingdom~135 + dominion~209 + authority~580 + angels/host/army~93 + marching~164 + subdue~322 + evil~270 + earth~291 + victory~781 + liberty~410 + rule~209 + reign~90 + finish~55 = **6,282**

God's universal purpose for mankind, stated in another way:

YAHWEH~26 + breathed~395 + dust~350 + created~203 + image~450 + likeness~160 + eternal~144 + spirit~214 + body~430 + begotten~44 + life~18 + obedient~410 + sanctified~404 + children~94 + unity~22 + blessed~222 + birthright~227 + build~57 + kingdom~135 + enter~9 + door~488 + *Shepherd*~275 + dwell~312 + garden~53 + eden~124 + Sabbath/rest~702 + forevermore~146 = **6,114**

Mankind's detailed purpose within *God's* universal purpose, stated in another way:

mankind~45 + birthright~227 + blessed~222 + name~340 + mark~406 + *God*~45 +

**Holy Spirit**~624 + <u>vessel</u>~60 + <u>image</u>~160 + <u>likeness</u>~450 + <u>eternal</u>~144 + <u>spirit being</u>~214 + <u>willing</u>~62 + <u>obedient</u>~410 + <u>begotten</u>~44 + <u>family</u>~433 + <u>circle</u>~17 + <u>household</u>~412 + <u>faith</u>~102 + <u>clothed</u>~332 + <u>white</u>~82 + <u>kept</u>~540 + <u>testimony</u>~79 + _**Word**_~206 + _**King**_~90 + <u>tongue</u>~368 = **6,114**

Resolution 6,114:

(6) mankind connected to **_God Almighty, El Shaddi_**

(1) first (purpose, creation, rule over earth)

(1) oneness with **_God_**

(4) gate to Eden opened, door to eternal joy

In **_Acts 1:8-9_**, we read that this <u>power</u> is given through **_Holy Spirit_** to become witnesses for **_Christ Jesus_**. _"But you shall receive <u>power</u> after that the **Holy Ghost** is come upon you; and ye shall be witnesses unto me both in Jerusalem, Judea, and in Samaria, and unto the uttermost parts of the earth."_ We have been given an assignment by **_Christ Jesus_** to use our birthright position of supernatural power to order angels to subdue devils. **_He_** has reclaimed for us this supernatural power. Each of us are to become one of the heroes in the faith as written of in the book of **_Hebrews_**. <u>Power</u> means…ability to work miracles, mighty works, strength, administrative powers, and ruler.

CHAPTER EIGHTEEN
THE BRIDE OF CHRIST IN REALITY

Now, to expound on the term, *Bride* of *Christ.* *Father God and Holy Spirt* have a *Son, Christ Jesus, Yehowshua.* *They* intend for *Jesus* to be happy and fulfilled like *They* are in *Their* marriage. When *He* comes to reign on this earth, *King Yehowshua* will have *His Bride, His* queen. *Scripture* has explicitly written of this fact. *Christ Jesus* spoke of this fact. *He* was not speaking in parables, but stating a reality, an event yet to occur. *Christ Jesus* was said to have despised the shame but did it for the joy set before *Him.* What are love stories made of? Usually, a movie plot goes like this; the hero is willing to risk his life for his lady. At just the right moment, the hero comes, steps in front of the damsel in distress, willing to take on the enemy's blows to protect her.

This theme throughout most stories is a good analogy of *Christ Jesus* coming in to rescue *His Bride*, though *He* indeed did take the blows and ultimately died for all mankind, not only *His Bride*. Yet, the thought of the joy set before *Him* was that *He* would wed *His* true love one day, as a flesh and blood man. Thus, the *Song of Solomon* is the most extraordinary love story ever told. Do you really think that section of the *Bible* only concerned a King's love for his queen? Or do you consider that book an analogy of *Christ Jesus* and *His* saved brothers and sisters? Why else would *God* have put this in *His Holy Word* if it was not part of *His* plan for this earth and the upcoming wedding feast? *(Song of Solomon / Hebrews 12:2)*

In *Scripture,* Jewish weddings were significant events in their culture, pointing to the future event that will undoubtedly take place for our *King* of kings with *His Eternal God Family. (Matthew 22:2 / Revelation, Chapter 19)*

Scripture verses highlight the importance of finding the perfect bride for every king in history. The details, rituals and time spent on this process were carefully thought out and dutifully performed. And too, the married couple was to have a full year to themselves; not do business, no labor for the married couple, but a lengthy honeymoon. The one-thousand-year reign on this earth will be *Christ Jesus'* honeymoon with *His Bride*. All of *God's* children will later be transferred to the city of New Jerusalem. We will live forever with *King Yehowshua* in mansions that *He* has promised to have been prepared once the honeymoon year (one-thousand-year reign) has been completed, and the devil is finally banished forever. *(John 14:2-3 / Revelation, Chapter 20)*

These types and shadows of the most ostentatious and festive marriage feast for *Yehowshua,* the *King* of kings and *His* devoted *Bride*, were played out in the lives of married spouses throughout the Old Testament. *Yehowshua* waits as *His Eternal Mother Holy Spirit* is here on the earth, completing these rituals and preparing *His Bride* while the whole world awaits *His* return to reign.

Much must be done beforehand. Children going into the millennial reign need to be set apart, sanctified, and taught in the ways of the *Lord*. The elaborate details of the *Bride*'s entourage, those wise virgins, her bridesmaids, must first be set apart as well as she readies herself for the wedding ceremony. As stated in *Scripture,* every jot and tittle must first be accomplished before this generation ends. *(Matthew 5:18 / Matthew 25:1-13)*

Eve was the physically embodied woman on earth who started this confusion and chaos with negative thinking, causing magnetically opposing forces to push away from *Holy Spirit*. For everything to come full circle, there must be a complete reversal of this negatively charged atmosphere. The proper actions, attributes and devotion must again be aligned with *God's* law and order of the eternal by way of another spiritual yet human, flesh and blood woman to right those wrongs. Bringing in our *Holy Spirit* in the fullness of *God's* kingdom come on this earth, the *Bride* of *Christ* will precisely accomplish that task. Not in her own strength or power, but as she submissively allows *Holy Spirit* to do this through her. Remember, we are created beings, not gods unto ourselves.

Christ Jesus fulfilled *His* part for the *Salvation* of mankind, and *Holy Spirit* indwelled *His Spirit* without measure. *Christ Jesus* remained entirely obedient in faith, having been taught and unquestioningly heeded faithful instruction spoken by *Father God's* '*still small voice.*' *Christ Jesus* believed the fullness of *Holy Spirit* was possible for *Himself* and a reality for *Their* created vessels of honor in order to live a sinless and obedient life while walking on earth. *Christ Jesus* was taken up the mountain for forty days while *He* wrestled with *His* flesh, ultimately denying *His* fleshly nature and accepted the indwelling of *Holy*

Spirit to see *Him* through *His* appointed commission and destined purpose while on earth. All of that *He* did in faith and trusting *God's* promises.

Within the realm of our reclaimed dominion authority, we are more than conquerors now because *Christ Jesus* conquered our sin and the devil's power over death. And *He* showed us the way to complete obedience and selflessness. *He* also exemplified *Holy Spirit's* full measure of help to be good, obedient, loving children of the living *Godhead*. The *Bride* of *Christ* will be *Holy Spirit's* representative, a spirit-filled woman, a human being, utilizing the reclaimed power forfeited in the Garden, by Eve, concerning dominion authority. Once again, mankind will take back charge of this earth and order angel hosts to subdue all creeping things on this earth. Thus, the *Bride* will be cleaning house as *Holy Spirit* instructs her.

Scripture and history show us beautiful pictures of Jewish brides, wedding feasts, and marriages. Love is seen between couples throughout the Old Testament and going into the New Testament. Abraham's wife, Sarah, was beautiful beyond her years. It stands to reason that the *Bride* for *Christ Jesus* will also be quite lovely, more so because of possessing beauty within her heart, overflowing with love for *God's* children.

Abraham, Isaac's father, told his servant to go to another country, searching for a bride for his son. The servant searching for a bride on earth is a type and shadow of *Father God* as *He* has sent *Holy Spirit* here to earth to search for the perfect, humble *Bride* for *Their Son*.

And as shown in *Scripture,* when Rebekah lighted off her camel, it was love at first sight. Rebekah came to Isaac, proving that the *Bride* will come to *Christ Jesus,* in all humility, acknowledging *Christ Jesus* as her *Savior* and *King*. This will not occur as in a rapture, pulled up and away. Nope. This will be her acceptance of *Salvation*, prepared for the wedding feast and willingly coming to meet her beloved *Savior*, when *He* returns to earth.

In traditional Jewish weddings, the bride receives a call initially, a shout by the men, the groomsmen, complete with trumpets, music and singing, as they come marching through the city streets. The bride and her bridesmaids will then go out to meet the groom's party. So too, *Scripture* shows us that the *Lord's* return will not be a silent, sneaking-off. Too,

Rebekah came riding in on camels, which are symbols for bringing gifts. Rebekah came with gifts for her husband, Isaac. The **Bride** of **Christ** will bring gifts in the form of beautiful children taught about the **Lord**. **Christ Jesus** will then lovingly take them, His very own creations, under His wing. *(Matthew 23:37)*

To clarify this point of children being presented to **King Yehowshua** at the beginning of the millennial reign, consider the multiple millions of unborn babies who have been mercilessly slaughtered with the implementation of so-called reproductive rights laws that are brutal killings of these innocents, no less. When the dead in **Christ** rise first, this event will include those children who were aborted before birth or killed outright for their body parts by evil scientists or blood-thirsty satanists.

Consider too; children aren't liable for their actions until they reach the age of accountability. The **Bride** of **King Yehowshua** will see to this, in faith, with **Holy Spirit** alongside, that children remaining alive on this earth will be set apart, hidden, and protected during the tribulation period before **King Yehowshua's** return. And too, the **Bride** of **King Yehowshua** and **Holy Spirit** will lovingly receive those children who are then resurrected upon **His** return. *(1 Thessalonians 4:16-17)*

Another married couple who is a type and shadow of things to come is Jacob and his bride, Rachel, whom he deeply loved. He agreed to work for her. Her father, Laban, insisted that Jacob labor for seven years for her hand in marriage. But Laban was cunning and pulled a switch on Jacob, sending the older sister, Leah, into the marriage feast. Jacob was forced into working another seven years for his beloved wife, Rachel. It seemed very cruel and devious on behalf of Laban. However, it was a testing time for Jacob to prove he could remain faithful, waiting for his true love, by fulfilling his agreement through to the end. Endurance is required for **God's** children; faith is vital when we do not yet see the result with our own eyes. Seeing this generation through to the end, waiting it out and not turning away is the test. *Jesus* cautioned all seven churches on the necessity of endurance when getting close to the end of this generation. *(2 Peter 3:8 / Revelation, Chapters 1-2)*

Here we see two parallels concerning the seven years. Jacob was compelled to work for his true love, Rachel. In the same respect, when it is all said and done, and the city of New Jerusalem will come from heaven, *Christ Jesus* will have labored for seven spiritual years for *His Bride*, seven thousand years on this earth. Too, those seven years that Jacob experienced represent the entire tribulation period, laboring in the fields of harvest, endurance, times of testing, waiting it out for the fullness of time and finally realizing the victory through *Christ Jesus.* The two witnesses will be walking this earth during the time of the wrath poured out on the heathens, but they will still refuse to repent of their evil deeds.

There will also be the beginning of sorrows. Could that be what we are experiencing even now, seven years of grief before that antichrist is revealed? With so much invasion of privacy and government control, could the end be getting near? With each passing day, we can be confident the time is getting closer to our *Lord's* return! Then, the tribulation will occur, and shortly after that, the wrath upon the heathen who refuse to repent and acknowledge their dependence upon *God Almighty*. But through it all, as stated earlier, with our *Holy Spirit Mother* residing inside *Her* vessels of honor, all will be protected on this earth and hidden away. This will transpire precisely as it occurs in Jewish wedding rituals, waiting for the *Groom's* call, our *King* of kings.

Queen Esther, referred to as beautiful, points to a relevant parallel to the *Bride*. There was a detailed search, and they held a contest of sorts to see who would win the favor of the King. Likewise, a *Bride* has been searched for and found here on earth for *Christ Jesus*. Esther listened, prayed, and heeded those instructions, saving her entire Jewish nation from extinction. As already stated, this *Bride* chosen for *King Yehowshua* will also play a significant role in end-times events, reversing the negative atmosphere by bringing in *Holy Spirit* in all *Her* glory! How will this be? By the *Bride* being infilled and overflowing with *Her* resident glory! *(Revelation 3:10 / Revelation, Chapter 12)*

Another woman in the Bible who stands out as well is Ruth. Her kinsman-redeemer watched over her and saw to her welfare and future. Boaz took her as his wife and loved her, so she did not remain a poverty-stricken, shunned widow. Boaz provided for his bride in a significant way. So it was that Boaz, a Jewish man, married Ruth, a Gentile woman, after seeing her in the field, and she found favor in his sight. She is now included in the family lineage with **Christ Jesus**. What a blessing that has been bestowed upon mankind for us to play our part and be actively included in the beautiful story of the **Eternal Family of God!**

Again, just consider that young woman, Mary. It's been researched that she was probably 13 to 14 years of age when Gabriel visited her. She was a willing vessel, full of humility, specially commissioned to carry **Christ Jesus** in her womb. Although she is not a deity, Mary does deserve a place of honor for her trust and faithfulness.

CHAPTER NINETEEN
BRINGING IN THE KING'S REIGN

The kingdom *Christ Jesus* is to reign over will be here on this earth. Jerusalem, the homeland of the Jewish nation, will remain the center of *His* kingdom rule. *Christ Jesus* created all on earth and is the rightful *King* to reign over all life. Too, *He* won the victory over hell, death and the grave and reclaimed the dominion authority granted to mankind over the earth. *(Revelation 1:18)*

Meleck Yehowshua is *His* title *(King Jesus),* and *He* will restore this earth as initially intended before Lucifer fell to earth and then nearly destroyed it. That is except for the Garden of Eden. Although, that serpent was allowed to enter the Garden to test Adam's and Eve's lack of willingness to obey *God.* However, there is no genuine faith until it is tested and proven active in a person's heart, soul, and spirit. *God Almighty* never tempts anyone with evil thoughts of lust. *He* will test mankind to verify whether they believe *His* promises are true, no matter how long it takes to come to pass. *(Psalm 26:1-2 / Psalm 139:1-2)*

Along with our *King* ruling on this earth, we, the *Family of God*, will also receive territories to rule on this earth. In the glorified form, we will rule by family tribes, as always intended, and like the rule was implemented for Adam and Eve before their fall from grace. *King Yehowshua* will once again implement the system of family governments that *Father God* instituted within the Garden and then later with the tribes of Israel. *Scripture* shows that we will be kings and priests ruling over kingdoms. We will have dominion authority reclaimed for mankind under the watchful eye of *King Yehowshua.* *(Daniel 7:27 / Revelation 5:10)*

The *Song of Solomon* shares much about the relationship between a husband and wife. And too, this book of love tells the story of *Father God and Holy Spirit* and *Their* devotion to one another. The *Song of Solomon* also shows the intimate relationship of spouses in the marriage covenant as most precious. Love is the positive, magnetic drawing force and reason for creating life. Love in marriage is for the continuance of life, i.e., children, within their ever-expanding love, creating more life. We truly are made in the image and likeness of the ***Eternal Godhead Family. They*** want more of us! This is true love! Solomon had penned beautiful poetry to his bride, whom he loved most. She was described as the lily of the valley and the rose of Sharon. Scholars say this can be said of the ***Lord,*** but it is evident that this refers to a bride when read in context.

The ***Son of God*** will have constructed a house prepared for ***His Bride*** and the children of ***God*** before ***He*** returns to the wedding feast. And this house will be located in Jerusalem. First, though, will be the honeymoon period on this earth for one thousand years.

Then, after that has ended on this earth, there will come the ultimate test, allowing the father of lies out of its prison one final time for the proving of mankind born on earth during the millennial reign of ***King Yehowshua***. The people born and living during ***King Yehowshua's*** millennial reign will see and hear ***Him*** like it was when ***He*** walked this earth the first time. Except, ***King Yehowshua*** will be transfigured in glorified form like ***He*** was on the mountain when ***He*** spoke with Elijah and Moses. It wouldn't be fair or practical not to do so since all others of mankind have had their testing periods to prove their loyalty and desire to be included in the ***Eternal Family of God. (Luke 9:29-32)***

Remember, we have been instructed to request in prayer for ***God's*** kingdom to come here on earth as it is in heaven. Possibly, we should sing it out loud when reciting the Lord's Prayer? Doesn't one's work go better with music? ***Christ Jesus*** went to build a house for us in heaven.   And all of heaven emanates like a musical!

The *King* brings gifts to *His Bride*:

Anointed~358 + ***King***~90 + ***Yehowshua***~391 + build~57 + city~280 + singing/shouting~300 + ***Bride***~55 + dwell~312 + family~433 = **2,276**

Mother Holy Spirit and *Bride* bring the gift of the united family to the *King:*

Mother~41 + hand~14 + ***Bride***~55 + enter~9 + clothed~332 + white~82 + household~412 + birthright~227 + love~13 + singing~341 + singing/shouting~300 + family~433 + circle~17 = **2,276**

This equation holds the truthful answer, Resolution 2,276 :

(2) union of the ***Bride*** with the ***Son***

(2) witness and manifestation of the sons of ***God Almighty, El Shaddi***

(7) completed perfection, eternity of rest with ***God's Eternal Family***

(6) mankind connected with ***Eternal Family, Holy Spirit, God, Yehowshua***

Revisiting three forms given for 'love' in the Hebrew language:

The first is #157 / 'awhav' to be lovely, to be a friend or one's lover.

The second form is #160 / 'awhavah' …to experience romantic love and loyalty.

The third form is #7474 / 'raah' …to be beloved, one's darling and the object of a man's love.

Revisiting this equation shows each form of the word 'love' fits in with the poetry in the Song of Solomon and refers to his bride:

SONG OF SOLOMON:

love/lovely, lover~8 + love/loyal, romantic lover~13 + love/darling, object of my affection~285 = **306**

wife = aleph~1 + shin~300 + he~5 = **306**

Let's recap:

- א For ***His*** good pleasure, ***God Almighty*** purposed ***His*** creation, earthen vessels, to implement the increase of ***His*** kingdom through the institution of marriage and aided by the infilling of ***Holy Spirit.*** However, this truth hasn't been widely heard of.

- א Noah saved mankind's legacy, once again beginning new generations of families living on this earth, though the rain had been unheard-of before.

- א Abraham, in faith, believed in a son and started the nation of Israel, though an elderly couple conceiving a child had been unheard of before.

א Moses secured freedom for the Israelite slaves in Egypt, two million people, though ten plagues in a row had been unheard-of before.

א Esther saved her nation, Israel, from destruction by the king's right-hand man, though undoing a king's decree had been unheard of before.

א Samson gave his life, saving his people from an evil government intent on taking over Israel's Promised Land by destroying the nation's entire government leaders all at once. His feat of strength had been unheard of before.

א Mary disregarded the risk to her own life, trusting **God Almighty** to keep baby **Jesus** safe, though not being stoned to death for fornication had been unheard of before.

The list goes on of the mighty men and women who listened to that *'still small voice'* and heeded the call to go out and do their part in this world, though what they had been asked to do had been unheard of before. So, too, it is happening again in this generation. Unsung heroes and heroines are doing their part to implement this millennial reign upon this earth. **Father God** knows them, has called to them and they are listening, heeding, and obeying.

This is occurring even now:

א The **Bride** is listening; **Holy Spirit** is speaking, instructing.

א Children are waiting to be rescued by the **Bride** under the direction of **Holy Spirit.**

א The earth is groaning, eager for the fulfillment of prophecy and the manifestation of the sons of **God** in the fullness of **His** time.

א Saints having their oil lamps lit will implement their dominion authority worldwide, ordering angel hosts to arrest and imprison devils. Many will do this by family tribes in unity with **God Almighty's** instructions.

א   With prophecy fulfilled, every jot and tittle, these obedient sons and daughters of the **Most High God**, will compel **Father God** to release **His Son, King Yehowshua**, to return to earth to end all evil influences, finally. Goodness, love, and unity will prevail for one-thousand years!

As written in the last chapter of **Revelation**, the **Spirit** and the **Bride** are seen together at the end of this generation. They speak the exact words in the unity of their desire for our **King** of kings to return quickly. All fulfilled prophecies will have been accomplished according to **God's** laws. *(Matthew 5:18)*

In the perfect language, Hebrew, **Holy Spirit and Bride** say, *"Come!"* in **Revelation Chapter 22**. There is no exact word or definition for come in the Strong's Greek Dictionary Concordance concerning the verses **Revelation 1:7 or 22:17-20**. And concerning **Matthew 24:27,** no words are found for coming in the clouds. Appearing is the closest word to the word coming used in these verses, and it is equivalent in meaning to the word return in the Hebrew Concordance. *(Psalm 6:4 / Matthew 25:31)*

Hidden away in the Garden of Eden, *Holy Spirit* and *Bride* call to *Yehowshua*:

Holy/Spirit~624 + *Wife/Bride/*qof~406 + sound~136 + Hebrew~282 + tongue~368 + *Son/King*~142 = **1,958**

His Eternal Holy Spirit Mother and **His Bride** call to **King Yehowshua** to return to right all wrongs, suspending the evil oppression of the father of lies.

Garden of Eden~177 + Hebrew~282 + *Wife/Bride/*qof~406 + household~412 + groan~151 + birthright~227 + **God Almighty's** government~12 + earth~291 = **1,958**

The whole earth groans for the household of **God's** family to receive their birthright and inheritance; and for **God Almighty's** royal, governmental families to reign with our **King** on this earth. *(Romans 8:17-23)*

King Yehowshua returns and subdues the father of lies. "Yes! I will return soon, Amen!"

I~61 + Hebrew~282 + return~308 + subdue~322 + devil~304 + reign~90 + rule~209

+ <u>earth</u>~291 + <u>Amen</u>~91 = **1,958**

(Our **King** of kings is eager to return, make everything right in this world, and celebrate with **His Bride.** And **He** even says, "Amen!" So be it, as **King Yehowshua's** family calls to **Him.)**

<u>Resolution 1,958:</u>

(1) We live in unity with **Father God Almighty.**

(9) **King Yehowshua** finishes **His** work and suspends the evil works of the devil.

(5) Behold! **Holy Spirit** breathes in us and grants us to eat of the tree of life.

(8) We experience new beginnings and new life in the new millennial reign.

CHAPTER TWENTY
THE CIRCLE OF EARTH AND HEAVEN ABOVE

Prefacing this chapter by quoting *Scripture* is the right way to address the matter of our earth being circular and heaven above us. God's *Word* is true and active, rightly dividing the truth. *"For the **Word of God** is quick, and powerful, and sharper than any two-edged sword, piercing even to the dividing asunder of soul and spirit, and of the joints and marrow, and is a discerner of the thoughts and intents of the heart." (**Hebrews 4:12**)*

We have established that *Wisdom* is speaking of *Holy Spirit* in the book of *Proverbs.* *"**Wisdom** hath builded **Her** house, **She** hath hewn out **Her** seven <u>pillars</u>." (**Proverbs 9:1**)*

Some might say that the word, <u>pillars</u>, refers to the seven spirits of *God.* But this is a literal word with corresponding definitions in Hebrew. <u>Pillars</u> mean... pillars, posts, and columns.

*"...for the pillars are the **Lord's,** and **He** hath set the world upon them." (**1 Samuel 2:8**)*

*"...the foundations of the world were discovered...." (**2 Samuel 22: 8 & 16**)*

Keep this word, <u>pillars</u>, and its meanings, in mind as you read this chapter.

There is no mention of *God Almighty* developing more than what the following *Scriptures* state as having been created; no multiple galaxies, planetary ball-like spheres, or other worlds were included in the first sentence in the book of *Genesis.* *"In the beginning, **God** created the heaven and the earth." (**Genesis 1:1**)*

Look at the words for the second verse. *"And the earth was without form, and void; and darkness was upon the face of the deep." (**Genesis 1:2**)*

<u>Form</u>... confusion, nothingness, formless

<u>Void</u>... emptiness, empty and void

<u>Darkness</u>... obscurity, darkness

<u>Deep</u>... secrecy and darkness

At the very beginning of **God's Holy Word,** these two **Scriptures** show what **God Almighty** created. And this is all that **He** did create. No major thing **He** made was left out of **Scripture.** Only later, the father of lies added other imaginary places to exist, such as planets, outer space, galaxies and even gravity. All were based on that nothingness, that obscurity, secrecy out past heaven and earth. Even elaborate observatories funded by governments admit that their high-powered telescopes cannot actually see those imaginary planets. They tout that insufficient light is reflected from star constellations and the sun to view those clearly. Yet, somehow, they expect the average person to accept that the moon can reflect light on a dark and dormant rock and dusty surface.

Since they admit viewing planets is not possible, how can we believe that ancient Greeks and stargazers saw what they wrote of thousands of miles up? Much has since been written of those Greek theorists and stargazers. How did their crude telescopes see that far away? And why did those alleged planetary spheres all have names of idol gods they worshipped? What spirits were they listening to?

Explorers and scientists researched the earth's shape and calculated its structure for hundreds of years. All archaic cultures, not in any way associated with or in communication with other peoples, having lived hundreds of years apart, determined this world is a circular surface, and heaven above has a definite protective covering over our world. Depictions by Egyptians, Mayans, Hebrews, and Navajos, among other cultures, show a protective ceiling-like dome covering the earth.

Obviously, this was not a collaborative effort by these nations and cultures. And still, the earth was illustrated in much earlier writings worldwide. Some show mountains protruding upward but not slanted on a curved surface. All show water above and below the earth. "*And **God** made the firmament, and divided the waters which were under the firmament from the waters which were above the firmament, and it was so. And **God** called the firmament heaven.*" Firmament means… the space above the earth. Heaven means… region above the earth, the expanse of sky. *(Genesis 1:1-8)*

As far back as 1773, the Antarctic Circle was breached by the explorer Captain Cook, who came upon a massive glacial ice barrier. (Consider the fact that the Antarctic Circle is still labeled a circle. Only modern scientists have shrunk that circle and made it into an imaginary line around an island of ice and penguins.) The voyage of Captain Cook took three years to complete, not because of ice hindering their progress but because of the distance they traveled while exploring a wall referred to as the ice rim. In the captain's log, Captain Cook documented nothing but a consistent wall of solid ice as his ship traveled in a circular path close to that glacial wall. Captain Cook logged 69,000 miles that they had traveled as they followed this glacial wall.

By all the modern calculations of scientists' interpretation of this world, this would have meant that voyage would have sailed over six round trip cruises around this earth. Yet, current calculations presented as fact have stated earth is a ball measuring around 24,860 miles. So? How intelligent were those scientists when creating this illusionary outer space Hollywood production of spheres and ever-expanding galaxies? They didn't even delve deep enough to make simple calculations match previous records. It is good to see that when individuals dig deep enough, they discover lost facts about real voyagers' explorations.

In the more recent history of exploration, Admiral Richard E. Byrd explored the Antarctic Circle and noted several of the same observations as Captain Cook. He mentioned a huge wall of ice that appeared to be continuous and wondered what might be beyond it. Mysteriously, he died soon after those interviews. Almost immediately, all nations agreed to a worldwide treaty. Why would this even happen? Nations that went to war with one another all held to that treaty. One exception may have been Hitler, and so Admiral Byrd had been commissioned to go and see what Hitler was up to on the Arctic Circle.

In recent years, others who learned of a collaborated effort by powerful governments have begun to speak out. Why would all nations do this and not any nation oppose it? The answer is simple: money, power, resources, and real estate. Subsequently, all nations have a stake in that exploration and have reserved a piece of this frozen circular ice wall. And there is another reason for this massive deception; that is, satanists, who are aligned with their father of lies, have plans (although these men are grossly deceived) to keep control of the earth. Even *Scripture* warns us of their arrogance, rejection of their *Creator,* and a selfish desire to have this earth as their possession. *(Revelation Chapter 17 & 20:7-10)*

Another question is, why were encyclopedias sold door to door? Their indoctrination of the masses began with mere lies of ever-expanding galaxies and planets that hung on nothing more than manipulative words. At the time, only a paper trail was possible, without computers or advanced technologies, along with special news reports and movie theater promo reels. This is no coincidence since words hold power; even the father of lies knows this. Peddling books of mere fabrications and fictional accounts, tall tales no less, in the only way they could, i.e., textbooks and encyclopedias, they left a convincing paper trail.

They diligently went about brainwashing millions, if not billions of trusting souls, to gain money for their pet projects of explorations of this world while falsifying a moon landing project. Now, it is done with faked videos using elaborate optics. Though these videos lack good quality and are filled with editing issues, many in the film industry can easily spot their flaws. It should not be surprising to learn that encyclopedias and classroom curriculums discarded the old, tried and true information of eyewitness accounts from journals, by Captain's Logs, complete with mapped-out charts, in favor of these pretentious, scientific results of intelligent stargazers with new and improved high-powered telescopes.

Consider any of the photos of space you have ever viewed; that round, bluish-colored earth far away is surrounded by blackened emptiness. How is it that if there are trillions of stars and humongous star constellations out in that wide open space, we are not given photos or videos of brilliant lights or reflections? How is it that cameras or videos catch a glimpse of the earth with nothing else around it but blackness, or at the very least, a light reflection from off in the distance? Because those photos have always been faked, made by cameramen and digital imaging in a studio setting.

Admittedly, nothing can be seen, so what NASA shows us is straight out of their imaginations, just like Hollywood. Why don't we see videos of the earth spinning like a top? Are cameras so advanced they can snap a photo that is not blurred, though the world is supposedly spinning? How is it we are only allowed to see a rounded flat earth photo? And only still photos, but no action shots and no videos? They take all sorts of videos of astronauts inside a space capsule. They take videos on the moon. But they can't seem to take a video of our earth spinning and rotating on an invisible but tilted axis?

And it is no coincidence that the change in school curriculum occurred around the same time that the idea of the evolution of animals, especially mankind, began to creep into classrooms within the pages of schoolbooks. These new findings concerning evolution ran the gamut from a conglomeration of amoeba and frog-like creatures to primitive cavemen and ape-like creatures, all evolving over millions of years. Has no one questioned their facts? Has no one seen these different explanations as contradictions?

Most artifact finds to prove their facts and archeological digs have since been utterly debunked for not being as old as they were reported to be and not being from any prehistoric bones they claimed or from any unevolved species of man. Yet, retractions of their so-called finds had never been widely reported in the news. Once they realized they could successfully fool the masses, they stopped at nothing to spread their disinformation, pointing mankind further and further away from *God's* truth of creation. Sadly, church leaders have not done their research to expose these numerous lies.

Surprisingly, also not reported, as recent as the 1950s, in studying this world and its surroundings, honest exploration resulted in discovering a dome-like structure in the sky. But that critical information in the form of several reports was stifled, to say the least. Though ironically, those forms are still archived. With the development of NASA in 1958, supposed innovations in exploring unknown galaxies and space were ramped up. Before NASA was said to have breached outer space, otherworldly forms as god-like beings or planets those mythical beings were said to live on were understood to be mere Greek mythology, nonsense, and idol god worship.

NASA continually publicizes significant advances and discoveries out in a vast expanse of space. Interestingly, the word <u>NASA</u> is found in Hebrew and the Strong's Concordance. And on this point, <u>nasa</u> means…deceived, to deceive, greatly deceived, beguiled, seize, utterly forged. How odd! It is no coincidence that the father of lies would use a Hebraic word for the widespread sharing of its lies like a slap in the face of *God Almighty* if it were possible.

NASA claims new planetary galaxies were found within the last 50 to 70 years and are all named after those Greek gods. What a coincidence! Also, information began popping up that some of these supposed facts originated with ancient discoveries by famous Greek scholars and stargazers. Don't you think these assertions and comparative names for planets are more than a little odd?

Falsified planets named after falsified idol gods leftover from Greek religious rituals and beliefs are very telling. But even odder still is the fact that we have never questioned those intellectual human beings called scientists, astronauts, and researchers. The average man has no reason to doubt the intellectuals, and there were no calculators at the onset of their deceptions to prove or disprove their exhaustive mathematical calculations. It was way beyond the scope of expertise for anyone because the circumference, diameter and general space exploration figures were newly learned, as NASA experts informed mankind of their most recent discoveries.

Weird, too, is that no one hears about pilots questioning the lack of continuity concerning flight patterns, destinations and landing procedures regarding this world's false diameter and circumference, let alone the spinning factor. Why do we not see the earth moving below when up in a plane? In relation to air travel, with the time it takes to fly to a destination, along with the speed a plane travels, the plane would have soared upward and then flown away from the surface of a spherical earth at 35,000 feet. And why are pilots instructed to tell us this whenever we are on a flight? If the earth was a sphere, according to the calculations of NASA's interpretation of the sphere's curvature, pilots then must need to circle back towards the earth ball to locate their destination. Then the pilots would need to drastically tip the nose of their plane straight down to land on a paved roadway on the spinning ball of earth. Does this not sound like some impossible feat that only fantasy movie scripts are made of?

Now, if the earth was a ball and immensely larger than they say has been calculated, where the constancy of the curved portion was so gigantic, there might not be such an issue with their numbers or flight patterns. However, since they used a much smaller diameter and circumference to arrive at the two resulting totals for the size and shape of the earth, flight patterns on a ball-like sphere do not hold water. By the way, neither would a ball hold water on the outside of its surface, nor on a placid, glassy-like body of water be possible.

Until recently, the blue-collar working class has never questioned, let alone calculated to determine how it is that a jet can fly high upward to 35,000 feet which are approximately 7 miles, or so they tell us, and then level off in a straight pattern, but then not be flying away from earth and then needing to circle back in order to plummet vertically downward to get back the earth ball to line up with locating their destination for landing. And all of that must be accomplished on a spinning ball, no less! Possibly, mathematicians or physics majors have discovered factual rebuttals to these unlikely feats but were shut up, in one way or another?

For decades, students have been taught that we are supposed to be rotating and revolving simultaneously on a tilted axis. All this is believed to occur at speeds that would spin anything off a surface in a nanosecond, especially if trying to stay situated on a rounded surface. Doesn't this defy the fundamental laws of physics? An object remains in motion until it is stopped by a specific force stronger than itself. Is gravity supposed to be that force to handle all of this spinning with differing levels of weight or density? Why doesn't any life form here experience some form of dizziness? If we are spinning, how does water remain perfectly still like glass in lakes, rivers, and even the oceans? Why is water always level and not tilting if on a sphere and spinning at the same time? One can easily visualize this with a glass of water that they have propped to one side. Swirling water in a glass causes a funneling effect, forcing water to cling to the sides of the glass. And on another point, how is it that wells and springs are underground almost everywhere we drill for water?

Addressing the gravitation theory, why are trees not constantly swaying if the earth is spinning? How do the tiniest specs of sand on beaches located around the world of this supposed spinning, rounded globe stay in place? How can equilibrium be accomplished with all of this supposed motion going on in this world? Wouldn't the effects of a gravitational force be required to be individualized for any piece of matter on this earth? In other words, wouldn't one grain of sand need far less gravitational pull than an elephant? So then, why do some objects not float upward? Why do some objects not remain plastered to the earth, unable to move? Ever been on a spinning carnival ride?

Aerodynamic mechanics and speed enthusiasts have learned that Mach-five travels five times faster than the speed of sound. How are we able to function at Mach-86? How did that flag stay in place on the moon at not float away when it wasn't weighted like the astronauts' suits and shoes? How did it wave in the air? What air?

And on the point of curvature, why do rockets always bend in a definite curve as they ascend? If they are heading directly upward into that great outer space expanse, shouldn't they disappear out of sight, climbing straight up? Without the firmament with water above the earth, as spoken of in *Scripture* many times, a rocket would be able to jettison vertically upward. Yet, we can easily visualize the curve. Why is that? Why is a rainbow curved?

So many questions, observations and technological advancements are now readily available for one to investigate; if only there were enough interested souls who want to gain factual knowledge of the true supernatural realm in which we live.

The evildoers, mainly the wealthiest elites in this world, have all been sporting a grand lie as their play their real-time game of monopoly with earth. They aim to control everything, including the few humans they want to exist here as trans-human robots. These evildoers use mankind for hideous experiments to thwart *God's* plans for *His* created beings. Their agenda is the exact opposite than what *Father God Almighty* offers us. As stated before, the father of lies has its demons attempting to imprison us and ground us to this earth, turning us into evil, controlled, and destructive robots. No wonder they've invented gravity; you can't see or explain it. They are desperate for us not to discover our ability to ascend from glory to glory or be transported from one place to the other, like the sons of *God* whom we are meant to be. Faith is all it takes to have this become a reality in our lives, faith in our *Creator* and *His Salvation* plan through *Christ Jesus.*

Like with the mystery still surrounding electricity, scientists simply say gravity is out there in our atmosphere. Where does it begin? Where does it end? How is it possible that planes, rockets, ships, cars, trains, humans, animals, and anything that moves avoid its pulling force in varying circumstances? Is gravity able to be displaced in some way? No, this is where electrical magnetism, density, and pressure come into the equation. Gravity is a wild illusion that the elites have played on the world.

Here on earth, we are experiencing magnetism, density, and pressure, not any form of a conjectural force labeled gravitation. Or, that force would cause objects to be plastered up against the ground on earth while other objects would float around like feathers in the wind. With medical advancements, it is now known that our bodies are electrically charged within every cell. And isn't it again so telling that the term gravitational force was discovered initially by those ancient Greeks, who were said to be the enlightened ones who discovered planets? What nonsense and forbidden things have we agreed to in the last 70-to-100-plus years? *"Thou shalt have no other gods before* **Me.***" (Exodus 20:3)*

Consider this, if there were ever-expanding space and galaxies, then that would make **God's Holy Word** untrue. Is the evil plan of these scientists and NASA also part of the father of lies agenda to alter mankind's thinking concerning **God's** creation and provision?

Of course! *"My people are destroyed for a lack of knowledge..." (Hosea 4:6)*

If ever-expanding space was a fact of science, then the heavens weren't established and secure. *"Who laid the foundations of the earth, that it shall not be removed forever." (Psalm 104:5) "Fear before Him all the earth, the world shall be stable, that it be not moved." (1 Chronicles 16:30)*

Did you know that many scientists are masons? Most astronauts are as well; all have taken oaths to abide by whatever they are told to do and say. What about our national defense, namely the Air Force? There are archived videos and several little-known videoed interviews of astronauts revealing a telling fact that they are all instructed to lie to promote this exploration. This is done to acquire fame and fortune for themselves, as well as massive amounts of income for NASA. And they do not lie very well either; find and watch some videos of retired astronauts.

In the multiple billions, taxpayers' money has gone to the exploration of trying to bust through the protective firmament covering this earth that **God Almighty** has created to keep us safe. We are paying for self-proclaimed intellectual geniuses attempting to destroy this covering just to see what is out there past it or to attempt to escape their end, hell itself. It's their arrogance and rejection of their **Creator,** the tower of Babel, all over again. They send up rockets to try and penetrate this covering. They can never accomplish that, but they do not care if they succeed in shooting a projectile through the firmament.

Could horrible effects of penetration of the firmament that **God Almighty** has created over us to protect us be included with those vials of woe? Is this the explanation for those woes opened at the end of this age, the consequences of their arrogance and pride, **God's** wrath, i.e., the very penetration of that protective dome-like firmament, even if a tiny hole is formed? Will **God** give them what they want and allow the firmament to be breached toward the end of this age? And by doing this, they could cause consequences with their own hand. Yet, we will be safe in the Garden. *(Revelation Chapter 12 / Revelation Chapter 16)*

Sadly, many are still living in deception, not realizing the truth of this contained universe, but living under the evil influence of the men and women who are masons/satanists. In their wisdom and pride, those greatly deceived satanists actually believe the ultimate lie that they are gods, autonomous, and equal to, or better than, the **One** true **God Who** created them. In their arrogance, they also have fallen for the deception that they can go to war with **God Almighty** and defeat **Him** for control of this earth. *"Pride goeth before destruction, and an haughty spirit before a fall." (Proverbs 16:18-19)*

The father of lies knows victory is not possible. Likewise, its minions, demons, and devils realize it is impossible. But since those creeping, invisible devils on this earth only know how to lie and do acts of evil, they have cunningly convinced many humans to consider themselves to be their own arrogant and autonomous gods. But they are fools to the greatest degree. They have been persuaded with lies by devils, the demon children spirits of fallen angels. *"And when **He** was come to the other side into the country of the Gergesenes, there met him two possessed with devils, coming out of the tombs, exceeding fierce, so that no man might pass by that way. And, behold, they cried out, saying, What have we to do with **Thee, Jesus, Thou Son of God**? art **Thou** come hither to torment us before the time?" (Matthew 8:28-29 / 2 Thessalonians 2:11)*

Why has the majority of mankind blindly trusted the science of alleged intellectual men and women? Their deception and trickery have been very effective in this highly fabricated lie concerning an ever-expanding vast solar system. Even the term solar system defies our **God Almighty** and points mankind in the other direction toward the idol goddess, sol. And isn't that the face of the idol goddess on those coffee mugs by those who own and operate that coffee company and hate the USA?

Even more sadly, most pastors, scholars and teachers have never researched the **Scriptures** deeply enough to prove the truth. However, it also occurred long ago when mankind, in prideful arrogance, greatly deceived themselves during the construction of the tower of Babel. At least those people understood that they were capable of reaching the top of heaven while hoping to avoid another flood. Were they convicted of their sin? Were they also attempting to escape their known world and exist apart from their **Creator**? And too, they believed they could remain cloistered together, though **God Almighty** had previously commanded them to disperse across the earth. As Solomon had written, with mankind, there is nothing new under the sun. **(Ecclesiastes 1:14)**

What an amazing relief to know that our **Father God** has everything planned for our protection! It is reassuring to know that no matter if one thousand may fall at our left side and ten thousand at our right, it shall not come nigh our dwelling place. To know that we know that **God Almighty** is for us, and no one can stand against us is a wonderfully settling fact. Earth is our home, and we are to pray that **God's** kingdom comes to earth as it is in heaven. **Our Eternal Mother** wants **Her** home to be peaceful and a haven of rest. This ethereal bliss and unifying peace that passes all understanding, by way of our **Eternal Mother Holy Spirit,** is this peace which will bring about complete rest upon this earth, no more wars, murders, or disagreements within families, no sadness, no illness, no pain. **(Psalm 91:7 / Matthew 6:9 / Romans 8:31)**

The following verses of **Scripture**, using Hebraic words and their definitions, prove that our **Lord God Almighty** created immovable earth for us to exist on. **He** has protected us with a covering. We are to live here. We are to remain here. Our beloved family members are waiting to be reunited with us in Eden. **Father God** and **King Yehowshua** will return and be reunited with **Holy Spirit** and us because of **Their** love, mercy, and forgiveness.

1 Chronicles 16: 30... *"Fear before **Him**, all the earth: the world also shall be stable that it not be moved."*

Earth... earth, world, inhabited lands, heaven, and earth

<u>World</u>… world, habitable part

<u>Stable</u>… to be steadfast, to be firm, fitted, set in order, set fast, standing, secure

<u>Moved</u>… shall not be caused to move, not totter

Psalm 93:1… *"The* **Lord** *reigneth;* **He** *is clothed with majesty; the* **Lord** *is clothed with strength, wherewith* **He** *hath girded* **Himself***; the world also is stablished, that it cannot be moved."*

<u>World</u>… world, habitable part

<u>Stablished</u>… steadfast, firm, set in place, fastened

<u>Moved</u>… shall not be caused to move, not totter, not out of course

Psalm 96:10… *"Say among the heathen that the* **Lord** *reigneth: the world also shall be established that it shall not be moved:* **He** *shall judge the people righteously."*

<u>World</u>… world, habitable part

<u>Established</u>… steadfast, firm, set in place, fastened

<u>Moved</u>… shall not be caused to move, not totter, not out of course

Psalm 104:5… *"Who laid the foundations of the earth, that it should not be removed for ever."*

<u>Foundations</u>… a settled place, a site, a dwelling place

<u>Earth</u>… earth, world, inhabited lands, heaven, and earth

<u>Removed</u>… shall not be caused to move, not totter, not out of course

If there were an ever-expanding outer space realm with stars and galaxies, then **God's Holy Word** would not be true because it would mean that the heavens aren't established and secure. And too, **Father God Almighty** has settled us on this earth, fastened the earth down, set it firmly in place, which makes it steadfast and secure. He has appointed this earth as our dwelling place to have dominion over it. The earth shall not be moved, and we shall not be moved once we become close associates with our **Eternal God Family.**

1 Samuel 2:8...." *He raiseth up the poor out of the dust, and lifteth up the beggar from the dunghill, to set them among princes, and to make them inherit the throne of glory: for the pillars of the earth are the* **Lord's***, and* **He** *hath set the world upon them.*"

Pillars... situate, foundational support, pillar

Earth... earth, world, inhabited lands, heaven, and earth

World... world, habitable part

Father God has set in place pillars below the earth. We are situated on a pier and beam foundation with water above and water below us. This is how it rains, for the most part, and this is why water is found for constructing wells from underneath this terra firma. Of course, **Christ Jesus** is our sure foundation for **Salvation.** Yet isn't it good to know that we will not ever lose our earth to some wild, out-of-control orbiting chaos, a climate change catastrophe, or a massive nuclear bomb from a crazed person that would blow us off the map? *(1 Corinthians 3:11)*

One other matter is hell. Why would **God Almighty** place hell in the lower part of this earth if so many other planets and galaxies exist in a wide-open space? Wouldn't it seem feasible that **God** would have used a separated space, far away and reserved for the evil ones? Since there is only this earth on which mankind exists, only one hell is located below. As **Scripture** states, we will rise in levels of glory, from glory to glory. And the devil and its minions will be grounded, literally, underground. *(Psalm 55:15 / Matthew 23:33 / 2 Peter 2:4)*

One final matter to settle is the only verse in **Scripture** that deals with the word planet. Judah had fallen into idol worship, and so Josiah, the king of Israel, had all that nonsense destroyed; the false worship of the false god baal (the father of lies) and false heavenly figures and statues all having been conjured up from out of their imaginations. "*And he (king Josiah) put down idolatrous priests, whom the kings of Judah had ordained to burn incense in high places in the cities of Judah, and in the places round about Jerusalem; them also that burned incense unto Baal, to the sun, and to the moon, and to the planets, and to all the host of heaven.*" *(2 Kings 23:5)*

Planets are merely imagined idols, not at all real; not rotating out in space somewhere.

All planets are nothing but the devil's magical illusions played on mankind. Like everything else that snake has done, twisting and contriving some things into what those are not and turning other things from what those are into fabricated things, yet, those are merely theories, fantasies, taking up residence within human minds. Look at the meanings for planets in Hebrew. <u>Planets</u>, in Hebrew, means...zodiac signs (<u>idol worship</u>), constellations (<u>actual stars within the one and only firmament</u>).

<u>Here is an equation proving *God Almighty's* creation and satan's deception:</u>

<u>Yahweh</u>~45 + *<u>Word</u>*~206 + *<u>Holy Spirit</u>*~624 + <u>breathed</u>~395 + *<u>Yehowshua</u>*~391 + <u>created</u>~203 + <u>birth</u>~271 + <u>water</u>~90 + <u>earth</u>~291 + <u>heaven</u>~390 + <u>firmament</u>~380 + (all) <u>life</u>~18 + <u>good</u>~17 = **3,321**

<u>devil</u>~304 + <u>satan</u>~359 + <u>snake/serpent</u>~358 + <u>false/evildoer</u>~340 + <u>liar</u>~29 + <u>steal</u>~55 + *<u>Word</u>*~206 + <u>witness/beth</u>~2 + <u>mankind</u>~45 + <u>sin</u>~418 + <u>captive</u>~307 + <u>worship</u>~313 + <u>unity</u>~1 + <u>idol</u>~130 + <u>gods</u>~86 + <u>planets</u>~77 + <u>earth</u>~291 = **3,321**

Revelation, Chapter 21:1-3, speaks of the new heaven and new earth that will come down from *God's* domain. And this includes the fact that the first heaven and earth will pass away. Again, only those two are mentioned; no other planetary spheres or galaxies are referred to in any way. And to that point, if *God Almighty* had created planets, none would be named after idol gods! Honestly, would *God Almighty* approve of those names contrived from Greek gods and merely from mankind's imagination?

Scripture says that *God Almighty* will dwell with us on the new earth. This is precisely like *He* had done before when *He* walked in the cool of the day in the Garden. If *God* was lightyears away, existing within a massive, expansive habitation, why does *Scripture* show that *He* will choose to live here on earth with us? The absence of any mention of planets, galaxies, gravity, outer space, or advanced, intelligent alien beings other than demon spirits proves we have a close and loving *Father God* waiting to be reunited with us here on earth and then, later on, the new earth.

We truly exist within a limited created space and atmosphere, although this earth is more than enough for us. In the '70s, one genius mathematician calculated that every person on earth, 6 billion at the time, would be able to fit into one city, Jacksonville, Florida. Our *Father God* has granted us more than enough land. *Scripture* also proves that we are the only beings *God* saw fit to create. *(Genesis 3:8 / Revelation 21:3)*

Proof of only earth and heaven only within *God's* creation:

Elohim~86 + *Spirit*~214 + espousal~463 + unity~22 + womb~61 + moved~288 + void~13 + *Messiah*~358 + created~203 = **1,708**

water~90 + circle~17 + earth~291 + firmament~380 + stars~48 + heaven~390 + sea~50 + established~74 + foundation~115 + pillars~236 + good~17= **1,708**

I~61 + *Yehowshua*~391 + *Messiah*~358 + *Shepherd*~275 + door~488 + kingdom~135 = **1,708**

CHAPTER TWENTY-ONE
THE LORD'S PRAYER

Christ Jesus was asked how we should pray, and *He* replied that we should pray this way. So many confirmations are within this perfect prayer and should be viewed as special blessings to all who trust *Father God* to answer their prayers. *(Luke 11:2)*

The *Lord's* Prayer, *Christ Jesus* taught us to pray to our heavenly *Father*:

Our *Father* who art in heaven:

aleph~1 beth~2 yod~10 nun~50 vav~6/ + /shin~300 beth~2 shin~300 mem~40 yod~10 mem~40 = **761**

Hey!/Behold!/Grace! <u>he</u>~5 + <u>perfection</u>~7 + <u>eternal</u>~144 + ***Spirits***~214 + ***Son/Yehowshua***~391 = **761**

(***Father God*** is in heaven with ***His Seven Spirits*** and ***Son, Yehowshua***.)

Hallowed be *Thy Name*:

yod~10 tav~400 qof~100 daleth~4 shin~300/ + /shin~300 mem~40 kaph~20 **= 1,174**

King~90 + <u>dominion</u>~209 + <u>authority</u>~580 + <u>Hebrew</u>/Ibree~282 + <u>love</u>~13 **= 1,174**

(The ***King*** speaks with all authority over the creation *He* loves.)

Thy kingdom come:

tav~400 beth~2 aleph~1/ + /mem~40 lamed~30 kaph~20 vav~6 tav~400 kaph~20 = **919**

oneness/<u>aleph</u>~1 + <u>wisdom</u>~73 + <u>liberty</u>~410 + <u>kingdom</u>~135 + <u>sing/shout</u>~300 = **919**

(***God's*** children will walk in wisdom and unity, and with liberty will sing and shout in God's kingdom come to earth.)

Thy will be done on earth:

yod~10 ayin~70 shin~300 he~5/ + /resh~200 tsade~90 vav~6 nun~50 kaph~20/ + /beth~2 aleph~1 resh~200 tsade~90 = **1,044**

Elohim~86 + <u>head</u>~501 + <u>household</u>~412 + <u>mankind</u>~45= **1,044**

(*God Almighty* is head over the household of mankind and *His* will prevails overall.)

As it is in heaven:

kaph~20 + aleph~1 + shin~300 + resh~200/ + /nun~50 ayin~70 shin~300 he~5/ + /beth~2 shin~300 mem~40 yod~10 mem~40 = **1,338**

Godhead/Divinity/gimel~3 + <u>likeness</u>~450 + <u>image</u>~160 + <u>light</u>~207 + <u>music</u>~510 + <u>love</u>~8 = **1,338**

(This earth will be filled with music and eternal spirit beings infilled with light.)

Give us this day our daily Bread:

tav~400 nun~50 lamed~30 nun~50 + vav~6/ + /he~5 yod~10 vav~6 mem~40/ + /lamed~30 cheth~8 mem~40/ + /cheth~8 qof~100 nun~50 vav~6 = **839**

<u>likeness</u>~450 + <u>birthright</u>~227 + <u>eternal</u>~144 + <u>life</u>~18 = **839**

(*Father God* will provide all of our needs because *Their* likeness is our birthright for eternal life.)

And forgive us our debts:

vav~6 + samech~60 + lamed~30 + cheth~8/ + /lamed~20 nun~50 vav~6/ + /aleph~1 tav~400 aleph~1 shin~300 mem~40 tav~400 nun~50 vav~6 = **1,378**

Yehowshua~391 + <u>willing</u>~62 + <u>heart</u>~32 + <u>earth</u>~291 + <u>slaughtered</u>~19 + <u>sin</u>~418 + <u>lost</u>~7 + <u>mankind</u>~45 + <u>forgiveness</u>~113 = **1,378**

(This is the <u>truth</u>; *Yehowshua* sacrificed *His* life, and *His* <u>finished</u> work on the cross grants whosoever will accept ***Salvation***. Those who have taken *God's* <u>name</u> will have unity restored with *God's Eternal Family* and have an open gate into eternity. *Yehowshua* was crowned *King* over all and sat down at the right hand of *God*.)

As we forgive our debtors:

kaph~20 aleph~1 shin~300 resh~200/ + /samech~60 lamed~30 cheth~8 + yod~10 mem~40/ + /aleph~1 nun~50 cheth~8 nun~50 vav~6/ + /lamed~30 aleph~1 shin~300 resh~200/ + /aleph~1 shin~300 mem~40 vav~6/ + /lamed~30 nun~50 vav~6 = **1,748**

Shepherd~275 + *Father*/ab~3 + **YAHWEH** ransomed~95 + family~433 + forgiveness~113 + blessing~222 + eternal~144 + birthright~227 + spirit being~214 + unity~22 = **1,748**

(Behold the blessings for eternal spirit-being-temples who love family, forgive others through *Holy Spirit* and dwell in unity, as salt and light to this world!)

And lead us not into temptation:

vav~6 aleph~1 lamed~30/ + /tav~400 beth~2 yod~10 aleph~1 nun~50 vav~6/ + /lamed~30 yod~10 daleth~4 yod~10/ + /mem~40 samech~60 he~5 = **665**

Mother~41 + *Bride*~55 + reign~90 + hidden~388 + angels~91 = **665**

(*Mother Holy Spirit* and *Christ's Bride* will be hidden, and we must contain the glory of the *Elohim*, have *Their* mark and name with the seven spirits of *God* and *Holy Spirit* for angels to hide us away with them, during the tribulation.)

But deliver us from evil:

kaph~20 yod~10/ + /aleph~1 mem~40 he~5 tsade~90 yod~10 lamed~30 nun~50 vav~6/ + /mem~40 nun~50 he~5 resh~200 ayin~70 = **627**

YAHWEH~26 + deliverance~130 + captives~307 + born~54 + new beginning in eternal life/heth~8 + faith~102 = **627**

(So be it! Because of our faith, deliverance is guaranteed for those the devil would make captive during the tribulation.)

For *Thine* is the kingdom and the power and the glory forever, Amen:

kaph~20 yod~10/ + /lamed~30 kaph~20/ + /he~5 mem~40 mem~40 + lamed~30 kaph~20 he~5 /+/ vav~6 he~5 gimel~3 beth~2 vav~6 resh~200 he~5/ + /vav~6 he~5 tav~400 pe~80 aleph~1 resh~200 tav~400 /+/ lamed~30 ayin~70 vav~6 lamed~30 mem~40 yod~10/ + /ayin~70 vav~6 lamed~30 mem~40 yod~10 mem~40/ + /aleph~1 mem~40 nun~50 = **2,012**

Father/ab~3 + eternal~144 + power~48 + dominion~209 + authority~580 + *Mother*~41 + *(Christ Jesus) Word*~206 + family~433 + Adam/mankind~45 + power~48 + life~18 + forevermore~146 + amen~91 = **2,012**

(Our **Eternal Mother,** with **Father God,** gives us eternal life within **God's Family,** so that we, being delivered and loosed eternal vessels by the sacrifice of **Christ Jesus,** are able to receive the mark and the name of **Father God Almighty** upon us. We receive power and dominion authority, granted through all authority of **Christ Jesus**, to go from glory to glory in **God's** kingdom forevermore!)

CHAPTER TWENTY-TWO
RAPTURE REFUTED

After expounding on mathematical proofs that verify the rest of this epic love story about our **Eternal God Family**, it might seem the thing to do would be to dismiss the topic of a rapturing away of the church, which everyone in the Christian arena agrees is not explicitly written out verbatim anywhere in the **Bible**. Likewise, verses that address a skyward meeting don't offer any fixed timeline for a secretive catching up and away in the course of end-time events.

One might suggest that if the previous context hasn't swayed a reader towards the whole truth of being hidden away on this earth during the tribulation and wrath, then it's futile for one to bother expounding on this point any further. Yet, the future safety, security, and peace of mind for all saints are of utmost importance to our **Father God.** So, it is necessary to address verses of **Scripture** that seemingly point many believers toward a conclusion of a rapturing in catching up and away.

As stated as plainly as possible, there will be hiding away for the children of **God.** Saints who have **His** name and mark on them will be taken to the Garden of Eden, according to **Revelation, Chapter 3:7-13 and Chapter 12:13-17 and 22:4.** Remember, <u>paradise</u> means…Garden of Eden, which **Christ Jesus** referred to when assuring the thief on the cross.

And then, in **Revelation, Chapter 12:6 and 14,** this occurrence, this hiding away, is this event written of in both verses. And yet, this wonderful event will appear as having been a rapturing away by those left remaining who are holding to the premise of and looking forward to a rapture. Thus, confusion, grave disappointment and even panic could result, as some might decide to turn away from **God,** thinking **He** abandoned those who claim to have been saved. However, for those true believers and saints of **God** who will remain behind, this is written for them to be greatly reassured! Those saints may be those commissioned by **God Almighty** to remain through the tribulation, witnesses enduring until the end, and for some even unto death, as it reads for those in the church of Smyrna. **(Revelation 2:10 and 12:11 and 12:17 and 20:4)**

In *Revelation 12:14,* this verse speaks to the fact of the hiding away and supernatural, angelic protection for **Holy Spirit** and **Her** children. *"And to the __Woman__ were given two wings of a great eagle, that **She** might fly into the <u>wilderness</u>, into **Her** place, where **She** is nourished for a time, and times, and a half time, from the face of the serpent."*

In *Revelation 12:17,* this theme continues, *"And the dragon was wroth with the __Woman,__ and went to make war with the <u>remnant</u> of **Her** <u>seed</u>, which keep the commandments of __God__ and have the <u>testimony</u> of __Jesus Christ__."*

This remnant are those saints commissioned to remain, being witnesses for **Christ Jesus**. This verse definitely pertains to Smyrna, those saints alive at the time of end-time events whom John's vision and writings refer to. This threefold cord, the **Eternal Family,** is named in these verses: **Woman/Her, God, Jesus Christ.** All three members of the **Godhead** are involved in the redemption of mankind's universal purpose on this earth.

Greek Concordance definitions are given:

<u>Wilderness</u>…a far-off out-of-the-way remote location; an unoccupied deserted place; a reserved, unique, and solitary place

<u>Seed</u>…children, offspring

<u>Remnant</u>…ones left, the rest of

<u>Testimony</u>…testimony and witness

Though Greek translators used the word <u>wilderness</u>, it has a greater meaning that explains a paradise and Garden located far from everything else on earth, i.e., hidden from view. And not to be overlooked, this verse also pertains to **Holy Spirit** and **Her** children hidden with **Her,** as well as those children who remain behind, all who have their testimony of accepting the free gift of **Salvation by Christ Jesus.** It is simply stated in this verse of **Scripture.**

Searching more in-depth certain **Scripture** verses, with **Christ Jesus' own words, He** shared detailed facts of **His** return. Still, those verses do not illuminate our understanding or resolve the varying points of view on this matter of either going through the tribulation, being taken in a rapture, or being hidden away on earth.

Written in the book of **Matthew, Chapter 24**, **Christ Jesus** speaks of the chronicled logistics of the end days. **He** referred to the beginning of sorrows but did not mention the exact period from the beginning of sorrows to our **Lord's** return. Verses 27 through 31 offer no clear signs of hiding away on this earth or a secretive rapture. Verse 29 merely addresses the tribulation ending at the point of our **Lord's** return. And most Christian denominations view these verses as a specific warning to the elect of the Jewish nation.

A diligent review of verses 29, 30 and 31 offers sure signs of a loud appearing, an angelic army host, a trumpet, and strange and unusual signs in the heavens. Also, the gathering of **His** elect from one end of the heavens to the other is listed there. Since those verses do not include any discourse on a *secret catching up and away*, those cannot be speaking of a rapture. One would be required to conclude that though **Christ Jesus** spoke on many details of **His** return, **He** didn't bother to address the church **He** had just established. It is not likely that **Christ Jesus** would exclude this one precious group eagerly awaiting **His** return: **His** faithful followers.

There is the truth stated of the gathering of **His** elect from one end of the heavens to the other. Yes, we will ascend upwards in the clouds; this is certain. As seen in previous chapters, those equations proved that we are eternally created spirit beings and will begin to rise above this earth with increasing levels of glory before our **Lord's** return. Remember, **Christ Jesus** had stated that we would do greater things than **He** had, and **He** was transported to safety, away from those who tried to stone **Him.** Others have indeed been recounted as having walked above the earth; even Peter had walked on/above the water. Maria Woodworth Etter, 1844-1924, was an evangelist, one in which **God** worked many miracles through her. Maria was reportedly known to remain in a state of suspension, above the stage platform, in the glorified presence of **God's Holy Spirit** for days on end. Newspapers of that time reported on this phenomenon. We will have the privilege to walk above the ground going from glory to glory before our **King's** return to earth because of amplified dominion power granted to us and resident within each of us.

We will experience the blessings of life in the supernatural eternal realm, being swiftly translated from one place to another, like Enoch, Elijah, Moses, and **Christ Jesus** experienced while in their physical, bodily forms on this earth. It seems we have a long way to go to get to this point in our sanctified existence. But **God Almighty** does things supernaturally and suddenly. Yet, for most, increased glorified forms will occur relatively close to the time we are whisked away to the Garden of Eden.

Consider this fact; in the days of Noah's flood, his family was safe within that ark; they remained on earth while all living creatures died in the massive and powerful flood. **Christ Jesus** also spoke to this fact for when He returns to the earth, the end-times events will be like in the days of Noah. What could be more dramatic or traumatic than the event of that flood, where the whole lot of creatures died on this earth all around Noah's family, and still, they were protected? Since **God Almighty** had Noah's family go through that harrowing experience, why do Christians consider it strange and unthinkable that **He** would cause us to stay on earth as the end-time events unfold?

And why do some think catching up and away is better, but being hidden away is a far less than perfect form of safety and security? When **God Almighty** oversees this event, there will be no glitches; all will be securely provided within the Garden. One question has to be asked. Who doesn't want to be present and eyewitnesses of our **King** of kings returning to earth in all **His** splendor and glory, with an angelic host accompanying **Him**? "*A thousand shall fall at thy side and ten thousand at your right hand, but it shall not come nigh thee.*" **(Psalm 91:7 / Matthew 24:38)**

Two other **Scriptures** address some Christians' premise of being raptured up into heaven or caught away into the upper atmosphere of the clouds during pre-trib or at least mid-trib. Many have deliberated on these verses as proof of a rapturing of the Church/believers. Paul, the apostle, penned both verses that cause some saints to cling to the hope of a rapture. He spoke of the same facts **Christ Jesus** had explained concerning **His** return. Paul also addressed our glorified form, meeting our **King Yehowshua** in the clouds. And in so doing, he referred to **Father God's** family members experiencing this glorified eternal realm. Nothing of the sort is mentioned about a secretive catching away.

1 Thessalonians 4:16-17… *"For the **Lord, Himself** shall descend from heaven with a <u>shout,</u> with the <u>voice</u> of the archangel, and with the <u>trump</u> of **God**; and the dead in **Christ** shall <u>rise first</u>; then we which are alive and <u>remain</u> shall be <u>caught up together</u> with them in the <u>clouds to meet</u> the **Lord** in the air, and <u>so shall we ever be with</u> the **Lord**."*

In the other verse that follows, Paul addresses the demise of the antichrist upon **King Yehowshua's** return. Again, he does not speak of a secret rapture. Paul's writings are a prelude to the verses of **Scripture** later written by John in **Revelations, Chapter 19.**

*2 Thessalonians 2:1…." Now we beseech you, brethren, by the <u>coming</u> of our **Lord Jesus Christ**, and by our <u>gathering together</u> unto **Him**, that you be not soon shaken in mind or be troubled, neither by spirit, nor by word, nor by letter as from us, as that the day of **Christ** is at hand. Let no man deceive you by any means, for that day shall not come, except there come a falling away first, and that man of sin be revealed, the son of perdition; who opposeth and exalteth himself above all that is called **God**, or that is worshipped, so that as **God** sitteth in the temple of **God**, shewing himself that he is **God**. Remember ye not, when I was yet with you, I told you those things? And now ye know what withholdeth that he might be revealed in his time. For the mystery of iniquity doth already work, only **He** who now letteth will let, until he (antichrist) be taken out of the way. And then shall the wicked be revealed, whom the **Lord** shall <u>consume</u> with the **Spirit <u>of His mouth</u>,** and shall destroy with the <u>brightness</u> of **His** coming. Even him, whose coming is after the working of satan with all power and signs and lying wonders, and with all deceivableness of unrighteousness in them that perish because they <u>received not the love of the truth,</u> that they might be saved."*

So, we can easily understand that the antichrist will be done away with when **Christ Jesus,** our **King** of kings, returns to rule and reign on this earth, and we will be with Him in the one-thousand-year millennial reign. *(Revelation 5:10)*

Greek Concordance definitions are given:

Shout…loud command, shout, signal, conspicuous, eye-catching, pronounced

Voice…voice, sound, speaking a language, noised abroad

Trump… trumpet

Rise... come back to life

Remain... to be left

Caught up... carried away, taken by force

Meet... meeting, encounter

Clouds... clouds

Ever be with... for evermore

Coming...(no definition found)

Gathering together... meeting, assembling together

Consume... destroy

Brightness... appearing, appearance

Spirit **of** *His* **mouth...** wind, breath, edge of the sword, *Holy Spirit* (*King Yehowshua* returns and speaks with power like *His Mother Holy Spirit.*)

This verse does not settle the issue of a raptured event in any way, so this verse should not be used in an attempt to confirm a teaching on a rapture theory. In breaking down the fundamentals, we discover that with the words: shout, voice, and trump, there is a definite lack of pointing to a silent secretive rapture, and points to quite the opposite scenario of everyone seeing this supernatural event take place, even those who received not the love of truth.

Concerning the word rise, this verse does not refer to going skyward. The definition literally means...coming back to life, being resurrected from the dead, i.e., coming out of the grave. The word, remain means...to be left here.

Ezekiel was also taken upward to see a vision that *God* wanted him to experience. He explained that he was between heaven and earth in this vision and transported to the inner gates of Jerusalem. *(Ezekiel 8:1-3)*

Paul spoke of a man, in or out of his body, who was taken up to the third heaven. Paul didn't understand or know for sure. Was this Christ Jesus? Had Jesus heard unspeakable words not lawful for a man to utter? Paul even stated that of that man, he would boast, but not of himself. *(2 Corinthians 12:1-5)*

Neither of these verses speaks to a secret and silent rapture, though many try to parallel those *Scriptures* with that premise. These verses are like trying to compare apples to oranges when contemplating a rapture. Ezekiel's and Paul's experiences merely explain the supernatural ways in which *God Almighty* deals with mankind at certain times for *His* purposes and our true hope of going from glory to glory as we are sanctified. *(Ezekiel 8:1-3 / 2 Corinthians 12:1)*

We should trust *God Almighty's* power and provision and know that we will be somehow taken and hidden away. *Revelation 3:10* should be immeasurably comforting in that we will be kept from the hour of temptation that shall come upon the whole earth, to try them that dwell upon the earth. Accepting *Salvation* that *Father God* offers will secure our blissfully joyous eternal existence.

So why does it matter so much to some saints that we leave this earth rather than remain here and be provided for and significantly protected? Remember, we are made from the dust of this earth; we belong here on earth. Yet, we are not to be grounded to earth, or to worship this earth, as the father of lies attempts to do by deceiving human beings; but to be over this earth, overseers, and subduing all, including devils.

God Almighty created us to exist on earth, and included within our existence is our *Eternal Mother's* indwelling in us for our continued blissful happiness. We are our *Mother's* children, and *Her* intoxicating *Spirit* of that ethereal new wine will keep us from considering, embracing, or doing any form of evil. When our spirits are filled with glory and perfection, and our minds are filled with happiness and joy, there will be no room for evil thoughts to enter. Remember, this perfection was lost when Adam and Eve ate the forbidden fruit. They proved we must have the seven spirits of *Father God*, *Holy Spirit*, and *Christ Jesus* to be more than overcomers.

It shouldn't seem unusual to consider that we spirit beings will be able to ascend into the clouds and yet remain within the atmosphere of earth, much like Philip had been carried away by the *Spirit of the Lord* to another town after sharing the Gospel with the eunuch servant. This form of transportation will be an everyday occurrence in our perfected supernatural state. *Holy Spirit* was with Philip on this earth after Pentecost, and *Father God's* precious *Holy Spirit* is here with us now and will remain until *King Yehowshua* appears. *(Acts 8:26-40)*

Although pretty amazing, angels will regularly make their presence known while ministering to us. *Scripture* references many times when angels ministered to *Christ Jesus. God Almighty* has done this numerous times with other individuals in the *Bible*: Elijah, Moses, Abraham, Sarah, Lot, Mary, Joseph, Paul, John, and Philip, which will also be a commonplace occurrence for us.

Reviewing verses in the Old Testament, Enoch and Elijah are referenced as having been previously raptured. These verses are used to point to the capability of mankind to ascend into *God's* heaven. This is a misconception. Why? *Christ Jesus* said, *"And no man has ascended into heaven, but **He** that came down from heaven, even the **Son** of man which is in heaven." (Genesis 5:24 / 2 Kings 2:1-11 / John 3:13)*

In *Genesis 5:24*…*" And Enoch <u>walked</u> with **God**, and he was not; for **God** took him."*

There are no words in Hebrew to fully answer the question if Enoch was raptured up to heaven. Why? Because the only actual Hebraic words from the above sentence in verse 24 are: Enoch, walked*, God.*

<u>Enoch</u>… follower

<u>Walked</u> … to travel with, to walk with, to fade away, to depart, to lead away

<u>God</u>… Elohim

In that verse, there is no clear visual description of Enoch's method of travel when he had been taken away. No mention of this type of travel is recorded in the New Testament. A complete explanation of Enoch's departure is simply not there. The closest reference is that *Christ Jesus* was seen going up, ascending in the clouds. However, we have the other verse that *Jesus Himself* said concerning no man going to heaven except the *Son* of man, and we believe *His* truthful words.

In *2 Kings 2:11...* "*And it came to pass as they still went on and talked that behold, there appeared a <u>chariot of fire</u>, and <u>horses of fire,</u> and parted them both <u>asunder,</u> and Elijah went up by a <u>whirlwind</u> into <u>heaven.</u>*"

Concerning Elijah's departure, we do have a tremendous visual to show us just how Elijah departed. Yet, Elijah and fifty others saw this occur. Later, though fifty men searched for three days, they never found him.

<u>Chariot of fire</u>... chariot

<u>Horses of fire</u>... horses

<u>Fire</u>...fire, flames, lightning, flaming hot

<u>Parted asunder</u>... spread out, separated

<u>Whirlwind</u>... storm, windstorm, tempest

<u>Heaven</u>... region above the earth, the heavens of this earth, combined into one meaning

Remember; these definitions are taken from the Hebrew concordance. The region above the earth does say that Elijah went up to *God's* heaven or the third heaven. And we have *Christ Jesus'* words saying that is not possible, only He has been to haven and went back to heaven. And too, we understand that flesh and blood cannot enter heaven.

In this verse, we learn that Elijah's taking up was not a silent departure; others saw him leaving in that miraculous way. Fifty men didn't even believe what they saw was an angelic, forcefully aided departure, so they went off to look for Elijah.

There is yet another reason there will never be a silent rapture or a way off in space heavenly experience for anyone, except for the *Son* of man, as *He* had explained.

Hopefully, this has cleared up preconceived notions of a silent, secret rapture prior to *King Yehowshua's* obvious and brilliantly visible return to earth. Remember, we are the clay, made from the dust of this earth and are meant to live here while our **Eternal God Family** comes here to join us. *"**Thy** Kingdom come, **Thy** will be done on earth as it is in heaven."* We were never destined to live in heaven but to live here on earth. Possibly some will visit heaven? That is **God's** call. However, this is why **Christ Jesus** is preparing a new city for us, New Jerusalem, since this old earth shall pass away after one thousand years. *(Matthew 6:10 and 24:35 / Revelation 21:1)*

SUMMARY

To address questions that you might pose as to the ultimate purpose of this book, and more to the point, what is hoped to be relayed in this book, the following points should clarify these objectives.

א The Hebrew language proves the love of **Father God, Christ Jesus,** and **Holy Spirit, Who** are indeed our **Eternal Family** to **Whom** we have always belonged, and through **Whom** we see the fulfillment of **Their Salvation** plan for mankind.

א **Holy Spirit** is female, our **Eternal Mother** and the **Wife** of **Father God Almighty, El Shaddi,** and we have always had eternal life within **Them.** Not that we fully comprehend this truth, but we trust this truth, because eternal is eternal, with no end and no beginning, this perfect, continuing family circle.

א We have been blessed to experience a real purpose for living on earth as earthen vessels, created to contain the flowing ethereal wine of our **Mother Holy Spirit** within the hierarchy of our own families, and being submissively obedient to **God Almighty, El Shaddi's** perfect will and purpose for us to live out… and in the family **Father** has chosen to place us in here on earth.

א Within our **Eternal Family**, ultimately, we will live in and experience eternity, in the fullness of the ethereal and blissful supernatural realm.

א Love and forgiveness are the keys to **God's** part of **His** creative venture on earth and building up **His** family in a greater way, as well as for our redemption. Too, love and forgiveness are our keys to everlasting peace for all mankind.

א **Christ Jesus gave His life and shed His precious pure blood for our Salvation. Christ Jesus** also reclaimed our dominion authority to subdue earth and every creeping thing on this earth.

א There will not be a rapture as most churches teach, instead, as we await the wedding feast, we will be hidden away.

א   Mankind dooms himself when using his free will not to accept his loving **Eternal Family**. **They** created him, an earthen vessel with an earthly purpose to fulfill, and then, to live with **Them** forever. But, by rejecting the truth of one's total dependence for even their very breath given by his **Creator,** mankind dooms himself. (Not to forget; those who have never heard the **Good News** of our **Eternal Family** reuniting us to them, will one day have their opportunity to accept being part of **God's Family** in the millennial reign, when **Christ Jesus** returns and resurrects them from the grave.)

א   Hebrew is the perfect language that only **God Almighty** could have made. Every letter, word, number, and subsequent meanings, point to creation, **Salvation** and our **Eternal Family's** love for us, **Their** children.

א   Hebrew was the only original language that had been spoken before **God Almighty, El Shaddi** leveled the tower of Babel, and will once again be the communicated language of **Father God's** children.

א   Hebrew is filled with mathematical equations, producing resolutions that prove the truth of the existence of our supernatural spiritual **Eternal Family, Who** have always kept us close to **Their hearts** as eternal spirits, and then did an even greater loving thing, by creating for us physical bodies; to fulfill **Their** ultimate purpose for more generations to come on this earth.

א   Many **Scriptures** prove the truth of the circle of earth and heaven directly above earth. This is the one and only universe that **God Almighty, El Shaddi,** has ever created. The earth is circular and on a foundation of pillars, not a ball-like sphere. Heaven is coming down here to us; we will not go up to heaven.

א   The Garden of Eden has been preserved and is reserved here in earth, for us who have come into the manifestation of our dominion authority, in faith, and who are clothed in white. And this is where our deceased loved ones are currently residing. Like those resurrected, God's children and **Yehowshua's Bride** will be caught up to meet **Him**! Initially, will be hidden away with **His Bride**, all will eagerly await

Christ Jesus, our *King* of kings, *King Yehowshua,* to return to rule and reign over *His* kingdom of earth.

א The falsified teaching of planets, galaxies, and ever-expanding space is a lie. Like with evolution, their scientific facts are lies; all is brainwashing.

א The devil is that father of lies, an entirely defeated foe, as with all its devils, demons, imps that roam this earth. Before being hidden away, we are to exert our reclaimed dominion authority over all creeping things on this earth, cleaning house with *Holy Spirit's* urging and guidance, making those enemies to be the footstool for *Christ Jesus.*

The pure, crystal-clear language, Hebrew/Ibree, entails the strong, threefold cord of words, letters, and numbers from *God Almighty's* mouth in *His* throne room. Combined with inspired *Scripture* written in Hebrew, this language confirms the absolute truth about creation and *God's* purpose for mankind. It adds up perfectly! God's *Holy Word* establishes your purpose!

God Almighty has written down everything that's on His mind concerning creation. *Father God* wrote down *His* good pleasure in Hebrew; this threefold, confirming, perfect language, and even included the plan for your life! There is a room of record books kept in heaven on everyone who has ever lived. Did you know there is one book with your name on it? In it has been written *His* pre-planned purpose for you, laid out like a blueprint for your life. And on those pages, records of what you have done with your life are kept. *(Psalm 139:16 / Revelation 20:12)* (The wrongs you've done have been mercifully blotted out; if you have repented of going your own stubborn way and have accepted *Father God's* loving forgiveness, through *Christ Jesus*.)

Father God takes great pleasure in seeing that your purpose is fulfilled. And thankfully, *He* has sent *Holy Spirit* here to assist you in accomplishing your purpose. Isn't it great to learn that we have help and do not have to do life alone? No matter how many struggles we are faced with, we have this hope to attain this extraordinary reality in the here and now. We have supernatural assistance in the form of love, counsel, comfort, knowledge, wisdom, and goodness. Our genuine expectation, to go from glory to glory, has already been planned for us to experience on this earth and throughout eternity.

Father God Almighty knows best; we should trust that *He* does. So long as we allow our thoughts to align with *God's* thoughts and our desires to go along with our *Creator's* desires for increased creativity on this earth, we will feel completely fulfilled and established. All our questions answered, no more stressing, not confused, no longer wondering what life is all about. We will attain the peace that passes all-natural understanding as we walk on this earth.

Don't be tied down to this earth by the devil's deceptive lies. Don't waste your valuable purposeful time here, during this dispensation, by looking for aliens and other planets to live on. We have the real ability to live here on this earth in glorified form, far above the deceptive form of an autonomous existence here on earth. Since time began, the father of lies has attempted to convince mankind that their only option, or best option, is an antichrist existence here on earth, or in outer space, which is merely a fabrication of multiple falsehoods.

God Almighty has always been willing to share secret details of *His* true-life story and plans when we care enough to spend time with *Him,* listening to that *'still small voice'* and then search it out. And this eternal, true-life story is the most extraordinary love story ever told! And wonder of wonders, you are included! You are always on *Their* minds and the recipient of *Their* love. *Father God* loves *Eternal Mother Holy Spirit.* And *They* love *Their Son, King Yehowshua.* This *Eternal Family* truly loves *Their* creation, mankind, so much so that *They* have sacrificed much and worked together to redeem mankind back to *Them.* Allow this threefold cord of love encircled in the presence of our *Eternal God Family* to wrap *Their* loving arms around you with perfection, purpose, and supernatural reality.

One day we will live in perfect peace in the holy city of peace, Jerusalem!

Hey! Behold! Grace!~<u>he</u>~5 + <u>begotten</u>~44 + mankind/<u>vav</u>~6 + <u>chosen</u>~210 + <u>qof/bride</u>~100 + <u>dwell</u>~312 + <u>Jerusalem</u>~586 + <u>city</u>~280 + <u>valley</u>~ 210 + <u>peace</u>~376 + kingdom/<u>yod</u>~10 = **2,139**

Israel~541 + chosen city~490 + valley~210 + seven-spirits of **God**~586 + dwell~312 = **2,139**

Christ/Messiah~358 + **King**~90 + heart~32 + chosen~220 + bride~55 + seven-spirits~586 + blessing~222 + begotten~44 + man/vav~6 + dwell~312 + valley~210 + gate/door/daleth~4 = **2,139**

Resolution 2,139:

(2) manifestation of the sons of **God,** our witness to faith in **Christ Jesus**

(1) complete unity with the **Eternal Godhead Family**

(3) **Divinity,** gifts given to the spirit, soul, and body

(9) mature character, finished work

"O praise the Lord all ye nations: praise Him all peoples! For His merciful kindness is great toward us and the truth of the Lord endureth for ever. Praise ye the Lord!" (Psalm 117)

Our hope is this reading has blessed you. More importantly, may these revealed esoteric truths fill your spirit, soul, and body with joy, while discovering these supernatural truths, giving you a deeper love for your **Eternal Family of God.** *(Acts 17:24-2 / 1 Corinthian 6:17, 19, 20 / John 14:16-17 / Acts, Chapters 1-2 / Genesis 1:28 / Matthew 23:37 / Matthew, Chapter 22 / Revelation 1:18 / Daniel 7:27 / Revelation 20:4)*

Bible references were taken from KJV Bible. Using Hebrew root words, definitions/meanings were taken from Strong's Concordance. Some references were used from the Greek section.

HEBREW LANGUAGE MATHEMATICS GLOSSARY

LIMITED WORD~to~NUMBER REFERENCE

ALEPH/**GOD** = Yahweh = yod~10 + he~5 vav~6 + he~5 = 26

ADAM/MANKIND = aleph~1 + daleht~4 + mem~40 = 45

AMEN = aleph~1 + mem~40 + nun~50 = 91

ANGELS = mem~40 + lamed~30 + aleph~1 + kaph~20 = 91

ARMY/HOST = tsade~ 90+ beth~2 + aleph~1 = 93

AUTHORITY = tav~400 + qof~100 + pe~80 = 580

BEGOTTEN = yod~10+ lamed~30+ daleth~4 = 44

BIRTH = men~40 + kaph~20 + vav~6 + resh~200 + he~5 = 271

BIRTHRIGHT = beth~2 + kaph~20 + resh~200 + he~5 = 227

BLACK = shin~300 + cheth~8 + resh~200 = 508

BLESS = beth~2 + resh~200 + kaph~20 = 222

BODY =nun~50 + pe~80 + shin~300 = 430

BREATHE = nun~50 + shin~300 + mem~40 + he~5 = 395

BRIDE = kaph~20 + lamed~30 + he~5 = 55

BLOOD = daleth~4 + mem~40 = 44

BORN = yod~10 + lamed~40 + daleth~4 = 54

BRUISED = daleth~4 + kaph~20 + aleph~1 = 25

BUILD = beth~2 + nun~50 + he~5 = 57

CAPTIVE = shin~300 + beth~2 + he~5 = 307

CHAOS/CONFUSION = beth~2 + shin~300 + tav~400 = 702

CHILD/SON = beth~2 + nun~50 = 52

CHILDREN = yod~10 + lamed~30 + daleth~4 + yod~10 + mem~40 = 94

CHOSEN = beth~2 + heth~8 + resh~200 = 210

CHOSEN w/special favor = beth~2 + cheth~8 + yod~10 + resh~200 = 220

CIRCLE/CIRCUIT = cheth~8 + vav~6 + gemel~3 = 17

CITY = ayin~70 + yod~10 + resh~200 + he~5 = 280

CLOTHED = lamed~30 + beth~2 + shin~300 = 332

COUNSEL = ayin~70 + tsade~90 + he~5 = 165

CREATE = beth~2 + resh~200 + aleph~1 = 203

CROWN = kaph~20 + tav~400 + resh~200 = 620

DAUGHTER = beth~2 + tav~400 = 402

DAY = yod~10 + vav~6 + mem~40 = 56

DEATH =mem~40 + vav~6 + tav~400 = 446

DELIVERANCE/LOOSED = he~5 + tsade~90 + lamed~30 + he~5 = 130

DEVIL = shin~300 + daleth~4 = 304

DOMINION = resh~200 + daleth~4 + he~5 = 209

DOOR =pe~80 + tav~400 + heth~8 = 488

DRAW= qof~100 + resh~200 + beth~2 = 302

DUST = ayin~70 + pe~80 + resh~200 = 350

DWELL = yod~10 + shin~300 + beth~2 = 312

EARTH = aleph~1 + resh~200 + tsade~90 = 291

EDEN = ayin~70 + daleth~4 + nun~50 = 124

ELOHIM = aleph~1 + lamed~30 + he~5 + yod~10 + mem~40 = 86

ENTER = beth~2 + vav~6 + aleph~1 = 9

ESPOUSAL = cheth~8 + tav~400 + nun~50 + he~5 = 463

ESTABLISHED = yod~10 + samech~60 + daleth~4 = 74

ETERNAL = qof~100 + daleth~4 + mem~40 = 144

EVIL = resh~200 + ayin~70 = 270

FAMILY = mem~40 + shin~300 + pe~80 + cheth~8 + he~5 = 433

FAITH = aleph~1 + mem~40 + vav~6 + nun~50 + he~5 = 102

FALSE/EVILDOER = resh~200 + ayin~70 + ayin~70 = 340

FATHER = aleph~1 + beth~2 = 3

FEAR (of the Lord) = yod~10 + resh~200 + aleph~1 = 211

FEED = resh~200 + ayin~70 + he~5 = 275

FEET = resh~200 + gimel~3 + lamed~30 = 233

FINISHED = kaph~20 + lamed~30 + he~5 = 55

FIRE = aleph~1 + shin~300 = 301

FIRMAMENT = resh~200 + qof~100 + yod~10 + ayin~70 = 380

FLED = beth~2 + resh~200 + cheth~8 = 210

FOREVERMORE = ayin~ 70 + vav~6 + lamed~ 30 + mem~40 = 146

FORGIVENESS = samech~60 + lamed~30 + yod~10 + heth~8 + he~5 = 113

FORMED = yod~10 + tsade~90 + resh~200 = 300

FOUNDATION = mem~40 + vav~6 + samech~60 + daleth~4 + he~5 = 115

FREE = he~5 + pe~90 + shin~300 + yod~10 = 405

GARDEN = gimel~3 + nun~50 = 53

GIFTS = mem~40 + tav~400 + nun~50 = 490

GIFT (YAHWEH RANSOMED) = pe~80 + daleth~4 + vav~6 + he~5 = 95

GLORY = kaph~20 + beth~2 + vav~6 + daleth~4 = 32

GOOD = teth~9 + vav~6 + beth~2 = 17

GROAN = nun~50 + aleph~1 + qof~100 = 151

HAND = yod~10 + daleth~4 = 14

HATE = sin~300 + nun~50 + aleph~1 = 351

HELL = shin~300 + aleph~1 + vav~6 + lamed~30 = 337

HEY! LOOK! GRACE! BEHOLD! (Breath of *Holy Spirit)* = he~5 = 5

HEAD = resh~200 + aleph~1 + shin~300 = 501

HEALING = resh~200 + pe~80 + aleph~1 = 281

HEART = lamed~30 + beth~2 = 32

HEAVEN = shin~300 + mem~40 + yod~10+ mem~40 = 390

HEBREW/IBREE = ayin~70 + beth~2 + resh~200 + yod~10 = 282

HIDDEN = cheth~8 + pe~80 + sin~300 = 388

HOLY = qof~100 + daleth~4 + vav~6 + shin~300 = 410

HOLY SPIRIT = (QODESH) qof~100 + daleth~4 + vav~6 + shin~300 + (RUACH) resh~200 + vav~6 + cheth~8 = 624

HOST/ARMY = tsade~90 + beth~2 + aleph~1 = 93

HOUR = shin~300 + ayin~70 + he~5 = 375

HOUSEHOLD (family/place of residence) = beth~ 2 + yod~10 + tav~400 = 412

I = aleph~1 + nun~50 + yod~10 = 61

IDOLS = samech~60 + mem~40 + lamed~30 = 130

IMAGE = tsade~90 + lamed~30 + mem~40 = 160

INSTRUMENT = kaph~20 + lamed~30 +yod~10 = 60

ISRAEL =yod~10 + sin~300 + resh~200 + aleph~1 + lamed~30 = 541

JERUSALEM = yod~10 + resh~200 + vav~6 + shin~300 + lamed~30 + mem~40 = 586

JOY = sin~300 + mem~40 + cheth~8 + he~5 = 353

KEPT = shin~300 + mem~40 + resh~200 = 540

KILL = shin~300 + cheth~8 + teth~9 = 317

KING = mem~40 + lamed~30 + kaph~20 = 90

KINGDOM = mem~40 + mem~40 + lamed~30 + kaph~20 + he~5 = 135

KNEW= yod~10 + daleth~4 + ayin~70 = 84

KNOWLEDGE = daleth~4 + ayin~70 + tav~400 = 474

LACK = beth~2 + lamed~30 + yod~10 = 42

LAMB = shin~300 + he~5 = 305

LAND/EARTH = aleph~1 + resh~200 + tsade~90 = 291

LANGUAGE = sin~300 + pe~ 80 + he~5 = 385

LIAR = kaph~20 + zayin~7 + beth~2 = 29

LIFE = cheth~8 + yod~10 = 18

LIBERTY = daleth~4 + resh~200 + vav~6 + resh~200 = 410

LIGHT = aleph~1 + vav~6 + resh~200 = 207

LIKENESS = daleth~4 + mem~40 + vav~6 + tav~400 = 450

LILY = shin~300 + vav~6 + shin~300 + nun~50 = 656

LOST = aleph~1 + beth~2 + daleth~4 = 7

LOVE (a friend or a lover) = aleph~1 + he~5 + beth~2 = 8

LOVE (romantic love, and loyalty) = aleph~1 + he~5 + beth~2 + he~5 = 13

LOVE (object of a man's devotion) = resh~200 + ayin~70 + yod~10 + he~5 = 285

MANKIND/ADAM = aleph~1 + daleth~4 + mem~40 = 45

MAGNIFY= gimel~3 + daleth~4 + lamed~30 = 37

MARCHING = tsade~90 + ayin~70 + daleth~4 = 164

MARK = tav~400 + vav~6 = 406 (*God's* mark/name in *Revelation 3*)

MARRIED = he~5 + yod~10 + he~5 = 20

MESSIAH = mem~40 + shin~300 + yod~10 + cheth~8 = 358

MIRACLE = mem~40 + vav~6 + pe~80 + tav~400 = 526

MOTHER = aleph~1 + mem~40 = 41

MOUTH = pe~80 + he~5 = 85

MOVED = resh~200 + cheth~8 + pe~80 = 288

MUSIC = shin~300 + yod~10 + resh~200 = 510

MY LOVE = resh~200 + ayin~70 + yod~10 + he~5 = 285

NAIL = yod~10 + tav~400 + daleth~4 = 414

NAME = shin~300 + mem~40 = 340

NEWS = shin~300 + mem~40 + vav~6 + ayin~70 + he~5 = 421

NOURISHED = kaph~20 + vav~6 + lamed~30 = 56

OBEDIENT = shin~300 + mem~40 + ayin~70 = 410

PEACE (SHALOM) = shin~300 + lamed~30 + vav~6 + mem~40 = 376

PERFECTION = tav~400 + mem~40 + yod~10 + mem~40 = 490

PERISH = daleth~4 + mem~40 + he~5 = 49

PIERCED = kaph~20 + resh~200 + he~5 = 225

PILLARS = mem~40 + tsade~90 + vav~6 +qof~100 = 236

PLANET = mem~40 + zayin~ 7 + lamed~30 = 77

PLEASURE = resh~200 + tsade~90 + vav~6 + nun~50 = 346

POWER = cheth~8 + yod~10 + lamed~30 = 48

PROPHECY = nun~50 + beth~2 + vav~6 + aleph~1 + he~5 = 64

PROPHETIC = nun~50 + beth~2 + yod~10 + aleph~1 = 63

PRAISE = he~5 + lamed~30 + lamed~30 = 65

PURE = teth~9 + he~5 + vav~6 + resh~200 = 220

QOF~100 = (Bride/Hebraic spiritual meaning) = 100

REGARD = nun~50 + sin~300 + aleph~1 = 351

REIGN = mem~40 + lamed~30 + kaph~20 = 90

REJECTION = mem~40 + aleph~1 + samech~60 = 101

REPENT = nun~50 + heth~8 + mem~40 = 98

RETURN = shin~300 + vav~6 + beth~2 = 308

RIGHTEOUSNESS = tsade~90 + daleth~4 + qof~100 = 194

ROSE = cheth~8 + kaph~20 + tsade~90 + lamed~30 + tav~400 = 548

RULE = resh~200 + daleth~4 + he~5 = 209

SABBATH (REST) = shin~300 + beth~2 + tav~400 = 702

SACRIFICE = mem~40 + nun~50 +heth~8 +he~5 = 103

SALT = mem~40 + lamed~30 + cheth~8 =78

SALVATION= yod~10 + shin~300 + vav~6 + ayin~70 + he~5 = 391

SANCTIFIED = qof~100 + daleth~4 + shin~300 = 404

SATAN = shin~300 + teth~9 + nun~50 = 359

SEA = yod~10 + mem~40 = 50

SEVEN = shin~300 + beth~2 + ayin~70 = 372

SEVEN SPIRITS=shin~300 + beth~2 + ayin~70 + resh~200 + vav~6 + heth~8 = 586

SHARON = shin~300 + resh~200 + vav~6 + nun~50 = 556

SHEPHERD = resh~200 + ayin~70 + he~5 = 275

SIN = cheth~8 + teth~9 + aleph~1 + tav~400 = 418

SING (SHOUT FOR JOY) = resh~200 + nun~50 + nun~50 = 300

SINGING = mem~40 + sin~300 + aleph~1 = 341

SKY = shin~300 + cheth~8 + qof~100 = 408

SLAUGHTERED = teth~9 + beth~2 + cheth~8 = 19

SNAKE (SERPENT) = nun~50 + cheth~8 + shin~300 = 358

SON (CHILD) = beth~2 + nun~50 = 52

SOUL = nun~50 + pe~80 + shin~300 = 430

SOUND = qof~100 + vav~6 + lamed~30 = 136

SPEAK = daleth~4 + beth~2 + resh~200 = 206

SPIRIT = resh~200 + vav~6 + cheth~8 = 214

SPOUSE = kaph~20 + lamed~30 + he~5 = 55

STAR = kaph~20 + vav~6 + kaph~20 + beth~2 = 48

STEAL = gimel~3 + nun~50 + beth~2 = 55

SUBDUE= kaph~20 + beth~2 + shin~300 = 322

SWORD = cheth~8 + resh~200 + beth~2 = 210

TEMPLE = he~5 + yod~10 + kaph~20 + lamed~30 = 65

TEMPTATION = mem~40 + samech~60 + he~5 = 105

TESTIMONY = ayin~70 + daleth~4 + he~5 = 79

THORN = qof~100 + vav~6 + tsade~90 = 196

TONGUE = lamed~12 + shin~300 + vav~6 + nun~50 = 368

TRUTH = aleph~1 + mem~40 + tav~400 = 441

UNDERSTANDING = beth~2 + yod~10 + nun~50 + he~5 = 67

UNITY = yod~10 + cheth~8 + daleth~4 = 22

VALLEY = ayin~70 + mem~40 + qof~100 = 210

VESSEL = kaph~20 + lamed~30 + yod~10 = 60

VICTORY = tav~400 + shin~300 + vav~6 + ayin~70 + he~5 = 781

VOID = beth~2 +he~5 +vav~6 = 13

WATER = mem~40 + yod~10 + mem~40 = 90

WHITE = lamed~30 + beth~2 + nun~50 = 82

WIFE = aleph~1 + shin~300 + he~5 = 306

WILDERNESS = mem~40 + daleth~4 + beth~2 + resh~200 = 246

WILLING = nun~50 + daleth~5 + beth~2 + he~5 = 62

WIND = resh~200 + vav~6 + cheth~8 = 214

WISDOM = cheth~8 + kaph~20 + mem~40 + he~5 = 73

WOMAN = aleph~1 + shin~300 + he~5 = 306

WOMB = beth~2 + teth~9 + nun~50 = 61

WORD = daleth~4 + beth~2 + resh~200 = 206

WORLD = tav~400 + beth~2 + lamed~30 = 432

WORSHIP = shin~300 + cheth~8 + he~5 = 313

YEHOWSHUA (*JESUS*) = yod~10 + he~5 + vav~6 + shin~300 + ayin~70 = 391

Find videos explaining the truths from Got Purpose

@ https://www.youtube.com/@yourkingdompurpose

Printed in Great Britain
by Amazon

13381413R00095